FAITH BEYOND HUMANISM

FAITH BEYOND HUMANISM

by DAVID RHYS WILLIAMS

Author of *World Religions and the Hope for Peace*

Introduction by

RABBI PHILIP S. BERNSTEIN

PHILOSOPHICAL LIBRARY

New York

In Memory of

My Parents

The Reverend David Thomas Williams
and
Esther Rees Williams

who gave life-long service in the Congregational Ministry
of America

My Grandparents

The Reverend William Rees
and
Theodosia Rees

who gave life-long service in the Congregational Ministry
of Wales

THE MYSTERY OF LIFE

The most beautiful thing we can experience is the mysterious. It is the source of all true art and science. He to whom this emotion is a stranger, who can no longer pause to wonder and stand rapt in awe, is as good as dead: his eyes are closed. This insight into the mystery of life, coupled though it be with fear, has also given rise to religion. To know that what is impenetrable to us really exists, manifesting itself as the forms—this knowledge, this feeling, is at the center of true highest wisdom and the most radiant beauty which our dull faculties can comprehend only in their most primitive religiousness.[1b]

—Albert Einstein

FOREWORD

So, you have lost your faith!

You can no longer subscribe to the set of religious beliefs in which you were reared. You have been disillusioned.

But you are not alone.

There are many formerly orthodox Protestants, Catholics and Jews who have had to discard much if not most of what they were taught about religion in their childhood and youth. Some have since achieved a dynamic faith of their own while others are still floundering about. To the latter this book is primarily addressed.

I, too, have gone through the experience of doubting and then rejecting almost everything in which I once believed.

Brought up in an orthodox home and church, I once believed in a God whom my imagination pictured as a majestic bewhiskered monarch, sitting on a high throne in heaven and recording in a huge book all that was happening on earth. Heaven was a city of golden streets and endless singing: Hell was a place of fire and brimstone and endless torture in a very literal sense. I was taught that to avoid Hell and make sure of Heaven logically should be the underlying concern of everyone's life, and that to proclaim this gospel was the most important work in which any one could be engaged.

At the early age of sixteen, I was greatly impressed by the life story of Dwight L. Moody, the distinguished evangelist. His obvious sincerity and sense of dedication inspired me to think of the ministry. My parents adopted a "hands off policy," but I could feel their unexpressed encouragement. When the decision was finally made to make the ministry my life work, I prepared for college with this objective in mind. While in college I was, of course, introduced to the study of science, philosophy, and comparative religion. Before the beginning of my junior year a book entitled *God and My Neighbor* by Robert Blatchford of England came to my attention. It proved to be a major turning point in my life. Suddenly the whole superstructure of beliefs which had housed my early youth collapsed about me. I found myself rejecting everything I had been taught about religion except its ethical precepts. It was the ethical aspects of my original decision to enter the ministry, fortified by the social vision of Professor Walter Rauschenbusch, described in his book on *Christianity and the Social Crisis*, which inspired me after graduation from college to go on to a theological school and thence to enter the ministry. The writings and speeches of such men as Dr. John Haynes Holmes, Dr. Harry Emerson Fosdick, Rabbi Stephen Wise, Mr. George W. Coleman of Boston's Ford Hall Forum, Dr. Algernon S. Crapsey, Mr. Eugene V. Debs, and Mr. Clarence Darrow were especially helpful in shaping the course of my thinking at that time. I remember that in my student days I volunteered to carry the suitcases of Rauschenbusch, Crapsey, Debs, and Darrow either to or from some meeting addressed by them in order to get a chance for a personal interview. My two older brothers were also vital factors in shaping my thoughts, as well as most of my professors in the theological school.

However, when I began my ministry, I possessed no theology worthy of the name, in spite of the fact that I had been given Bachelor degrees in both sacred and systematic theology. I continued to have a vague belief in Deity but I was at a loss to explain my belief. At any rate, this was my predicament when I launched into the active work of my profession.

I confess that all the arguments for the existence of Deity, which I studied in my college and seminary days, left me still unsatisfied.

There is, first of all, the famous argument from design. A sailor, stranded on a remote island, discovers a watch lying on the sands of the seashore. He picks it up and observes the perfect working of all its different parts; how every wheel and spring and screw and jewel conspire to achieve one common end, namely, to measure the lapse of time. Such a perfect subordination of means to an end could not have been the result of accident. It presupposes a watchmaker. Therefore, this stranded sailor comes to the conclusion that some intelligent being must have been responsible. By the same token the intricate ordering of this universe, where sun and moon and stars and planets gear into one another to form one stupendous whole, presupposes some watchmaker, some cosmic watchmaker; therefore, God exists.

Now the trouble with this argument, it seems to me, is with its major premise. Is this universe a perfect piece of mechanism? What about the element of accident and chance? What about the problem of evil? Do tidal waves and floods and earthquakes, which sometimes overwhelm whole cities and destroy the good with the bad, show evidence of design, and if so, what kind of design? Therefore, this argument to many is not entirely convincing. It was not convincing to me.

There is, secondly, the argument from practical experience. It is the pragmatic argument. If an idea works, it must be true. We have been told by the scriptures, "Whosoever doeth the will of the Father in Heaven shall know of the doctrine." In other words, practice the presence of Deity, act as though God does exist, and certain beneficial results will follow such as come in no other way. The idea of God works; therefore, God must exist.

Now the critics of this argument question its logic very seriously. They say, "Suppose you were to act on the theory that you had a rich, benevolent, elderly uncle in Australia and that some day you were to inherit his entire fortune. That belief would undoubtedly tend to relieve whatever anxiety you might now have for your future economic welfare, and perhaps give considerable present peace of mind. It might even inspire you to live more extravagantly and more adventurously than you can now afford, but it certainly would not prove that you had a rich, benevolent, elderly uncle in Australia." The pragmatic argument, therefore, leaves much to be desired. I found it unconvincing.

There is, thirdly, the argument from special revelation. For example, Moses claimed to have had an interview with

Deity at the scene of the burning bush, and again on Mt. Sinai when he was entrusted with the Ten Commandments; and the prophet Ezekiel insisted that the Almighty had given to him a special communication in a dream; and the Apostle Paul contended that on the road to Damascus a voice from Heaven spoke to him in clear and unmistakable language. Socrates went to his death, among other reasons, rather than deny that he was in daily touch with his guiding daemon. Mohammed, Joan of Arc, Swedenborg, and many other distinguished figures in history made similar claims of special revelation.

How can anyone brush aside the testimony of such distinguished eye and ear witnesses? How can one dispute the sincerity of those who proved their sincerity by the saintliness of their lives? Is not the positive testimony of one honest witness of more significance than a mountain of negative circumstantial evidence to the contrary? Perhaps so; perhaps not. It all depends on whether or not our honest witness could be mistaken in what he thought he saw or heard. For example, one can be honest and sincere and still be the victim of hallucinations due to epilepsy, or to an ecstatic condition arising from a prolonged period of fasting, or from some other abnormal physical condition. The argument from special revelation, therefore, has not been fully convincing to many because such mystical experiences are so rare, so uncommon, that they raise the question of their objective reality. This was certainly true in my own case. When I left the seminary, there was a large question mark after the argument from special revelation.

In the fourth place, there is the argument from the universality of belief. All races and peoples of all kinds and times have believed in some kind of God or Gods; not all have claimed special revelation, but all have claimed belief. Now it is argued such overwhelming testimony must be proof positive of God's existence. One individual here and there might very well be deceived, but how could billions of people down through the centuries have been led so far astray? But why not, answer the skeptics. Billions of people down through the centuries have believed in a flat earth and a sun that daily travels around this earth. Billions of people have believed in witches and demons and for many dark centuries the greater part of the world believed in the practice of offering human sacrifices to the gods. The universality of belief, therefore, is not necessarily any evidence of the truth of that belief. It seems to many that such logic leaves us precisely at the point where we began, namely, still begging the question, "What evidence is there for the existence of a spiritual universe?" At any rate, as I began my ministry I had no clear answer.

I decided to put theology on the shelf, so to speak. The subject had become peripheral in my scheme of things. It was the social application of ethical religion which almost wholly engaged my attention throughout the early portion of my ministry. The intervening years, however, have brought about a drastic change in my point of view. Not that I think less of the importance of the social application of ethical religion than formerly, but that I now look upon theology as the science above all sciences, as it was once so regarded in most intellectual circles for at least eighteen hundred years of western history. Not that theology has now or ever achieved the status of a science but that its subject is the most fundamental area of inquiry.

In spite of an initial resolve to put the subject on the shelf, the people to whom I ministered made it necessary for me to take it down from the shelf from time to time. I found myself again and again obliged to ask such questions as these: What experience common to all people has given rise to the concept of Deity? If the bibles of all religions were lost, would man sooner or later be impelled to reconstruct the concept anew? In short, what is God that man has been mindful of him? What did Voltaire mean when he said that if God did not exist man would be obliged to invent him? Is God nothing more than an abstraction at the end of a formula, or is He a present power in our daily lives? If a power in our daily lives, is this power personal or impersonal? If personal, what about the problem of evil? If God be good and all powerful, how can the presence of pain, suffering and injustice be explained? When Susan B. Anthony was about to leave for an extended tour of Europe, some one said to her,

"May God go with you." "O, He will," she is reported to have replied, "One can not get away from Him." [1] What kind of a God could she have had in mind? The late Archbishop Temple of Canterbury once declared, "It is a mistake to assume that God is primarily interested in religion." [1a] What concept of Deity must have been his to inspire such a challenging statement?

Here are some questions to which I have found partial answers which have meaning for me and may have for others. In this book, I attempt to identify the reality in man's experience which has put the word "God" into his vocabulary and then proceed to discuss some of its implications. I shall be interested to learn what reactions and criticisms these chapters may stimulate in the minds of you who read them. Throughout the book the word "spiritual" is used to include intellectual, emotional, aesthetic and ethical values. That is to say, all intellectual values are spiritual but not all spiritual values are intellectual.

I am indebted to Dr. Jacob Trapp of Summit, New Jersey, and Professor James Luther Adams of the Harvard Divinity School for encouragement and valuable suggestions. My thanks also go to the following Rochesterians for counsel and assistance in preparing the manuscript—Miss Florence B. Chillson, Miss Dorothy Dennis, Miss Ruth M. Harper, Mrs. Mary Decker Smith, Mr. James R. Davidson, Mr. Wallace Rust, Mr. Sterling Weaver and Mr. John A. Wenrich.

David Rhys Williams
Highland Parkway
Rochester, New York

CONTENTS

PART III—MEDITATION

INTRODUCTION

by PHILIP S. BERNSTEIN, D.D.,
Rabbi, Temple B'rith Kodesh, Rochester, New York

The religious liberal walks a tight rope in these times. On the one side are the revolutionary changes in man's thought and experience which makes so difficult the retention of faith based on reason. The Copernican revolution lowered man's status in the universe. Darwin demonstrated his animal descent. Freud revealed that he wasn't even responsible, consciously, for his conduct. Modern warfare has reduced the individual to insignificance, as it may pulverize him to nothingness.

If the individual turns the other way he confronts the rising tides of theology and ritual, of existentialism, escapism, and obscurantism. He sees how men turn away from the hard realities of life to "pie in the sky." A liberal minister finds it growingly difficult, in the religious sphere, to get men to *want* to do what in orthodoxy they *have* to do.

Timid souls may turn back. But the true liberal still heeds the ancient word, "Command the children of Israel to go forward." He knows that precisely in such times his liberalism is needed. Also needed are moral courage and intellectual integrity.

David Rhys Williams is such a religious liberal. For over a quarter of a century he occupied the pulpit of the historic First Unitarian Church in Rochester. In the nearly thirty years of our association I have never known a man with greater moral courage, with more rugged individualism, nor with more singleminded devotion to prophetic idealism. He has espoused more unpopular causes than any other clergyman in Rochester, perhaps more than all of them put together. He loves a good fight and would rather be attacked than flattered.

This book is his *apologia pro fide mea*. He writes of faith, his faith, lost and found. There is no retreat from reason, no escape to the esoteric, no flight from responsibility. He writes, "Our liberal theology looks well only when it walks arm in arm with liberal sociology." His faith in man, his devotion to human rights and civil liberties, his hope for peace, emerge as shining lights from a reading of the book. Also his tolerance. He writes with equal appreciation of the Catholic mass and of honest agnosticism. He does not evade even such difficult themes for a liberal as sin, immortality, and psychology. All are related to his concept of God growing out of the realities of human experience.

Evidence of wide reading and ripe wisdom are to be found on almost every page. And also an amazingly lovely and serene quality in the Meditations with which the book closes.

FAITH BEYOND HUMANISM

Part I

ARGUMENTATION

CHAPTER 1

THE GOD OF NATURE'S WONDER

There is at least one subject that in all probability will command the attention of the human mind when much of what is generally considered important today has long since been forgotten. It does not require any stretch of the imagination to believe that a hundred years hence, or a thousand years hence, men and women will still be talking about the concept of God. In these chapters I shall attempt to identify that reality in human experience which has given rise to this concept and then discuss its implications. My approach will be more psychological than theological and this I say, knowing well that I am neither a psychologist nor a theologian, except as every parish minister must be something of both in order to perform his parish duties acceptably.

The problem before us is most clearly stated in the Book of Job. "Then answered Job and said: Oh that I knew where I might find him, that I might come even to his seat! Behold, I go forward, but he is not there; and backward, but I can not perceive him; on the left hand, where he doth work, but I can not behold him. He hideth himself on the right hand that I can not see him. He goeth by me and I see him not. He passeth on, also, but I perceive him not." [2]

Whether you and I believe in God or not, it is a fact that a large portion of mankind, from earliest times down to the present hour, has been convinced that this world is inhabited by a personality transcending anything that the human eye has ever seen. For thousands of years the spirit of man has been disturbed by a presence which he has felt, but which he has never been quite able to locate or describe. "Oh that I knew where I might find him," has been the cry of many a sincere soul, down through the ages.

In spite of all efforts to disillusion him; in spite of all his failures to bring this presence within the compass of one or more of his five senses; in spite of all temporary misgivings and doubts, man has clung tenaciously to the thought that he possesses an unseen companionship in this world—more intimate, more sustaining and more vital than any companionship which he enjoys with his fellow human mortals or with his animal co-residents on this globe. When asked to define this presence, whatever other words he has used, he has always used the word "power."

What is this presence? It is a power which enables him to keep up his courage when his world begins to tumble in on him;

It is a power which enables him to resist temptation, and "pass by on the other side;"

It is a power which brings comfort to him in times of sorrow and bereavement;

It is a power which makes him reach out for things which appear to be beyond his grasp;

It is a power which seems at times to be underneath like an everlasting arm;

It is a power which fills his life with meaning and purpose when he yields his will to its influence.

When asked to locate this power, the mind of man has been bewildered and perplexed. Like Job, he says, "Behold I go forward, but he is not there, and backward, but I can not perceive him."

His prevailing inclination, however, has been to point to some object *outside* of himself. He has pointed to some belching volcano, and uttered the name of his Deity in awe and reverence, insisting that its cloud of smoke by day and pillar of fire by night were none other than the fingers of an Almighty One. He has pointed to the radiant sun as the seat of the presence which he felt within his own life, and when he drew pictures of the sun he painted friendly hands at the ends of the sun's rays. Some of these pictures adorn the temples of Egypt to this day.

In some ages, when asked to locate the reality which has

come to be called by the name of God, man has nodded in the direction of the sea, and uttered the name of Neptune. Or he has looked up to the moon and the stars in the heavens, or he has confidently ushered his inquirer into the presence of some totem pole, or graven image; or he has taken him into some temple of imposing architecture, and pointed to an altar with its consecrated bread and wine; or he has looked vaguely in all directions and said, "God is everywhere."

Each and every one of these efforts to locate Deity has satisfied the human mind at various periods in history, and millions of people throughout the world today are still satisfied with one or more of them. The modern mind, however, finds them all unsatisfactory. We understand now that physical energy is behind the belching of the volcano and the radiating warmth of the sun. We know today the chemical composition of the moon and stars. Our most powerful telescopes have searched out every corner of the heavens, and can not find there any evidence of a spiritual companion to man. All that our astronomers can see are molten suns and whirling stars and immense masses of luminous vapors—nothing but matter and evidence of physical energy, and vast inter-stellar spaces with apparently nothing in them, not even matter or the marks of physical energy.

There is force there in the heavens—there is awe-inspiring space there—there is inexorable law there, but surely there is nothing even remotely resembling the intimate and friendly spiritual qualities which man has ever associated with Deity—at least, nothing there that can be identified as such. There is no ethical personal power there—nothing worthy of man's love and devotion. Such a power may really be there, but if so, it is completely hidden from us.

Where then is God? If we can not find him with the telescope in the vast realm of infinite space, perhaps we can find him with the microscope in the realm of the infinitesimal. Perhaps we can locate him in the physical laboratory. But no, all efforts of scientists to date have failed to uncover any evidence of Deity in the world of the microscope. There are chemical and physical changes there; there are whirling points

5

of energy there; there are complex patterns of matter there, but who can feel inspired to bow down and worship before complex patterns of matter and whirling points of energy?

Where then is God? Is he to be found in the providential bounty of Mother Nature? In the variegated life of the changing seasons? Is there not a companion in the hills, "from whence cometh our help?" Is God in any of the striking phenomena of Nature? Says John Burroughs, "I see the Nature Providence going its impartial way. I see drought and flood, heat and cold, war and pestilence, defeat and death besetting man at all times, in all lands. I see hostile germs in the air he breathes, in the water he drinks, in the soil he tills. I see the elemental forces as indifferent toward him as toward ants and fleas. I see pain and disease and defeat and failure dogging his footsteps. I see the righteous defeated and the ungodly triumphant—this and much more I see." [3] No! There seems to be no partiality for moral or spiritual values in the ways of nature.

And yet, the ways of Nature constitute a large part of worship among all religions, including our own. The God of Nature's wonder is the object of extensive praise and adoration in both the Old and New Testaments, but especially in the Old Testament. We are told in the Nineteenth Psalm that:

> The heavens declare the glory of God;
> and the firmament sheweth his handy-work.
> Day unto day uttereth speech, and night
> unto night sheweth knowledge.
> There is no speech nor language, where
> their voice is not heard.
> Their line is gone out through all the earth,
> and their words to the end of the world.[4]

Again in the Eighth Psalm, it is the God of Nature's wonder that is extolled:

> O Lord our Lord, how excellent is thy name
> in all the earth! who hast set thy glory
> above the heavens. . . .

6

. . . . When I consider thy heavens, the work
of thy fingers, the moon and the stars,
which thou hast ordained;
What is man, that thou art mindful of him?
and the son of man, that thou visitest him?
For thou hast made him a little lower than
the angels, and hast crowned him with glory and
honour.[5]

It is still the God of Nature's wonder to which Jesus
directs our attention when he bade his disciples to

Consider the lilies of the field, how they grow,
They toil not neither do they spin,
And yet I say unto you that
Even Solomon in all his glory
Was not arrayed like one of these.[6]

There is no question but that a mysterious power must lie
behind all the phenomena of nature. It seems to be beyond
our capacity to comprehend. It fills us with awe and
reverence.

But, *is this power to be identified with* the God of ethical
religion? What ethical discrimination does it ever show? The
lightning of Nature's God strikes down the property of the
righteous as well as that of the wicked. His hurricane topples
over the steeple of a sanctuary of worship as recklessly as it
destroys the resort of folly. "He maketh his sun to rise on the
evil and the good, and sendeth rain on the just and the unjust," [7] as Jesus himself once said. In fact, as someone has so
well observed, "He sendeth more rain on the just because the
unjust have stolen the just's umbrellas." No, there seems to be
no moral awareness in the ways of Nature.

In the spring of 1912, the most palatial ship built up to that
time confidently steamed westward from England with the
port of New York City as its destination, when it suddenly
struck a huge iceberg. Many will recall the tragic fate of the
Titanic. Among the thousands on board, there were certainly
hundreds who prayed to be saved from a watery grave. Many

were saved, but more were drowned in the depths of the sea. Among those who were saved, there was much thanksgiving to God. But what about those who were not so saved? Were they less worthy than those who were rescued? Did the God who rules the winds and waves show any fine discrimination between the wicked and the righteous on that occasion? Surely whatever ethical discrimination was involved was certainly concealed from the comprehension of the finite mind of man.

Jesus came to a similar conclusion when an earthquake toppled over the Tower of Siloam and killed eighteen bystanders. "Suppose ye that . . . those eighteen upon whom the Tower in Siloam fell and slew them, were sinners above all men that dwelt in Jerusalem? I tell ye Nay." [8] And then he goes on to add, "But except ye repent, ye shall likewise perish," which seems to me to be an obvious non-sequitur. For even if all those eighteen had repented, they would have perished just the same.

If earthquake and tidal wave, if sunshine and rain, lightning, flood and forest fire, as manifestations of Nature's God seem to be indifferent to the survival of moral values, where then did man get his concept of a Deity so concerned? For answer, let us turn to a clue suggested by the experience of the prophet Elijah, when he fled from his enemies to take refuge on Mt. Horeb which was called the Mount of God.

> And he came thither unto a cave, and
> lodged there: and behold, the word of the
> Lord came to him, and he said unto him,
> What doest thou here, Elijah?
> And he said, I have been very jealous for the
> Lord God of hosts: for the children of Israel
> have forsaken thy covenant, thrown
> down thine altars, and slain thy prophets with
> the sword; and I, even I only, am left; and
> they seek my life, to take it away.
> And he said, Go forth, and stand upon the
> mount before the Lord. And, behold, the Lord
> passed by, and a great and strong wind

rent the mountains, and brake in pieces
the rocks before the Lord; but the Lord was not
in the wind: and after the wind an earthquake;
but the Lord was not in the earthquake:
And after the earthquake a fire; but the
Lord was not in the fire: and after the fire
a still small voice.
And it was so, when Elijah heard it, that he
wrapped his face in his mantle, and went out,
and stood in the entering in of the
cave. And, behold, there came a voice unto him,
and said, What doest thou here, Elijah?
and he said, I have been very jealous for the Lord,
the God of Hosts; for the children of Israel
have forsaken their covenant, thrown down
thine altars and slain thy prophets with
the sword; and I, even only I am left; and they
seek my life, to take it away.[9]

Now it is obvious that the prophet felt very sorry for himself. He was utterly discouraged. He was at the end of his own moral and spiritual resources. But it was then he heard the voice again which said unto him:

Go, return on thy way to the wilderness of
Damascus. . . .
and Elisha the son of Shaphat of Abelmeholah
shalt thou anoint to be prophet in thy room. . . .
So he departed thence and found Elisha the
Son of Shaphat who was plowing with twelve yoke
of oxen before him. . . .
and Elijah passed by him and cast his mantle upon him.[10]

Now, what was it that Elijah heard when he stood in the entrance of the cave of Mt. Horeb and which he describes as "a still small voice"? Was that voice Elijah's own or was it the voice of some presence other than that of Elijah? Surely Elijah must have been under the impression that he was hearing a voice entirely different from his own, otherwise we are

9

at a loss to account for the remarkable change that suddenly took place in his own spiritual state. Here is a man, utterly discouraged, who becomes full of confidence once more. Hopelessly paralyzed to the point of inaction, he is aroused to go forth and do something about his predicament. From a man mired in his own self-pity, he is changed into a dynamo of energy and renewed purpose. What was it that brought about such a drastic transformation? Was Elijah's experience something special and unique, confined to him only, or do we have here an experience common to all men and women?

According to Elijah's own testimony, the God he found, who brought him ethical insight and spiritual company, was not the God of Nature's wonder. Elijah did not find God in the great wind or the earthquake or the fire, but in some other manifestation of his presence.

The point which I wish to stress is that the God of Nature's wonder is not the source of man's sense of justice and mercy, or his awareness of truth, honor or any other ethical value. The God of Nature's wonder is full of majesty and power, but it is a physical power, prolific and bountiful and providential. Yes, but seemingly unaware and indifferent to pain and suffering or the survival of good and evil.

This God may fill us with joy and gratitude for the beauty and bounty of creation or with fear and awe at his wrath and chastisements, but surely he is not one to be prayed to with any confidence that our prayer will be heeded. "He watches the sparrow's fall," and seems to do nothing to prevent the falling of the sparrow. He watches the struggle of truth and falsehood, of freedom against oppression, of righteousness against unrighteousness and does not seem to intervene.

Clearly this God is not the God of ethical religion and can not be identified as such, except by deliberately shutting one's eyes to the facts of life and saying, "God's ways are past finding out. His thoughts are not man's thoughts," or, as William Cowper expressed it,

> Judge not the Lord by feeble sense,
> But trust Him for his Grace.
> Behind a frowning providence

10

He hides a smiling face.
Blind unbelief is sure to err,
And scan his work in vain.
God is his own Interpreter
And He will make it plain.[11]

Only by going against the known facts of life and taking a leap of the imagination can one attribute moral discrimination to the God behind the wonders of Nature. Let me honestly confess that my mind can not take that leap. Certainly not at this point in the argument. But I can sincerely respect the intelligence of those who are able to do so. Now mark you, I do not deny that moral discernment is one of the attributes of Nature's God. I deny only that man's experience with nature is the real origin of his concept of an ethical Deity, and affirm that this concept must come from quite a different experience.

In the next chapter I shall discuss that experience and attempt to identify the "still small voice" which Elijah claims to have heard.

CHAPTER 2

THE GOD OF COMMON EXPERIENCE

The wonders of nature can not be the real source of man's concept of an ethical Deity because the God of Nature seems to show no ethical discrimination. Therefore the ancient query posed by Job, "O that I knew where I might find Him!" still remains to be answered.

If an ethical God can not be found in the ways of Nature, where then did man get his idea of a Deity who is concerned with the triumph of good over evil, justice over injustice, and truth over falsehood? Where did he get the notion of a Deity who is at all interested in him? How did he come to hit upon the thought that he possessed the companionship of an unseen presence? Have such astute minds as Job and Isaiah, Plato and Maimonides, Augustine and Roger Bacon been completely deceived by their own imaginations? Has religion been talking and organizing all these centuries about something that has no basis in fact? Is God nothing but a passing fancy in the mind of man—an illusion of wishful thinking? Or is there some solid reality in the experience of the human race to which he can point as the unmistakable source of his God idea?

To answer these questions we must first ask, "What is it that we are looking for? What kind of presence is it that we are endeavoring to locate?" Surely it is something spiritual, is it not? Something that is other than ourselves; something that is greater than ourselves; something creative and purposive; something which cares for moral and spiritual values, which is able to support us when everything else fails; something which is able to offer us companionship when all others desert us.

Can such a spiritual power be found anywhere in the uni-

12

verse? I believe the answer to be an affirmative one. In man *himself* there is a dual life between which, in his more discerning moments, he is able to differentiate. There is a life which he identifies as himself, in referring to which he uses the first personal pronoun, and another life which he identifies as something other than himself, though directly apprehended by himself, in referring to which he feels he must use the third personal pronoun, except when he addresses it directly, when he inclines to the use of the second person.

Now this other life within man is the reality which has given rise to his concept of Deity. It embraces the whole spiritual phenomena which are involved in the process of faith.

Where others use the expression "Faith in God" I would say "Faith Is God." I make bold to identify Deity with the power of faith which projects ideal ends on the screen of man's imagination and then impels man to reach out and endeavor to make those ideals real. Even though I hold that "Faith Is God" there will be times when it will be more convenient to use the expression "Faith in God" just as we use the expression "the sun sets" when we know that it is the earth that circles the sun.

The affirmation that faith is God was inspired by Professor William James of Harvard. I was reading one day his description of the mountain climber who had worked himself into a position from which the only escape was by a terrible leap across a yawning abyss. He showed how faith makes a real difference in the facts of life. The mountain climber was able to believe that he could make the terrible leap and his feet were thereby nerved to its accomplishment. If he had disbelieved, but in a moment of despair had launched himself, he would have gone down into the abyss. "Our faith beforehand in an uncertified result is the only thing that makes the result come true." [12]

When I read this and its implications dawned on me, it came as a revelation to my mind. HERE IS GOD—here in the very act of faith is the creative factor of the universe. Here is the power that changes possibilities into actualities. Here is the dynamic that makes something out of nothing.

13

Here is the wondrous originator of that which is new, which makes a difference in the facts of life.

Furthermore, it seemed logical to me to hold that God can not be the object of faith—God must be the fact of faith. The object of faith is not a fact but always a possibility. If God were the object of faith, he would have to be a possibility and not a present reality.

No, what we are looking for is a spiritual creative power acting in the present. Here in the phenomena of faith itself, it seems to me we have that reality which we are looking for. In other words, the mysterious power which we experience as faith is none other than the Deity at work within us.

Nowhere does Professor James make this precise identification as far as I can learn. Several poets and hymn writers seem to do so, such as Martineau, Longfellow, Hosmer and Scudder. But most philosophers and theologians fail to make this identification, and their failure is due, in my judgment, to the fact that the world has long been accustomed to think of faith as a faculty of the human mind which can be exercised or not at will. Consequently the philosophers and theologians have been reluctant to identify such a power with Deity. It would amount to saying that man is God and this would be equivalent to saying that there is no God at all. But the obstacle in our path is in thinking of faith as a faculty of the human mind.

Professor William James speaks of the "will to believe." The Christian church during the Middle Ages hounded people to death for their failure to believe. The Christian church still holds people accountable for their beliefs. Even Jesus chided the people of his day for possessing little faith, as though faith were an achievement of the will. But I submit to you that wherever belief amounts to faith, it is not something that men can deliberately lay hold of and use at their discretion, but something that lays hold on them and uses them for its own ends. It is not something which serves them but something which they must serve.

That is to say, if one really believes in something, there is an appropriate reaction, but if there is no reaction, then there has been no real belief. Belief and behavior, faith and works,

14

are so intimately and vitally related as cause and effect that for all practical purposes they are one and the same.

Now at this point I want to make a distinction between faith on the one hand and fancy on the other, for faith and fancy are poles apart. Faith is not under our control. Fancy is. Let me employ a homely illustration.

When I was about nine years of age, I was taken ill with a severe case of measles and with the measles came an anvil-chorus headache. It was so bad that it seemed that my head was going to split apart. My parents comforted me with the announcement that the best doctor in the city, famous Dr. Sloan, was on his way to see me. I had heard about Dr. Sloan from my playmates and I certainly awaited his arrival with almost breathless expectation.

When he appeared by my bedside, he greeted me in a quiet but reassuring voice and then ceremoniously placed a strange looking little glass tube into my mouth. I know now that it was nothing more than a thermometer for reading temperatures. But since that was my first experience with a thermometer, certainly the first I can remember, I thought it was the magic wand that was to make me well again. And marvelously enough as Dr. Sloan gently placed it in my mouth, my headache magically disappeared. My faith was so complete that it must have brought about an immediate relaxing of nervous and muscular tension, which in turn relieved the pain in my head.

Recently when I was rushed to a hospital because of a heart attack, I had a severe pain in the region of my heart and arms. Even after morphine injections, it was so severe that when the head nurse came to take my temperature the next morning, I suddenly recalled my childhood experience and resolutely decided to recapture the naïve faith of my childhood, if possible. I made a conscious effort to believe that the thermometer would at least make some difference. But, when it was placed in my mouth, did anything happen? Nothing at all! There was no magic release from pain. I really did not expect that there would be.

In the first instance, my childhood belief was real. It was not an act of my will. It amounted to faith. It was, therefore, a dynamic factor which brought about an appropriate reaction.

In the second instance, my belief was not real. It was an act of deliberation and it amounted to a passing fancy and nothing more—a dilettante attitude—and therefore brought about no change in my physical state.

Just so, I contend there is a vast difference between a dynamic religious faith on the one hand and a dilettante fancy on the other. Whether God be clothed with the attributes of personality, or viewed as a spiritual principle, he must be accorded objective existence within the human imagination before he can become a relevant factor in our lives.

This process of objectivication necessarily takes place within the human imagination, but it is never a deliberate effort of the imagination. It is something that goes beyond our conscious knowledge but never against our conscious knowledge. The moment man becomes aware of the fact that the God he worships has been created by his own imagination, that moment he ceases to worship. Man must be possessed with the conviction that the God he worships exists objectively, otherwise he can not accord him supreme allegiance and devotion. He may let his fancy play with thoughts of the good, the true, and the beautiful. He may conjure up in his mind a wondrous ideal. He may even go through all the forms and ceremonies of outward religious worship. He may audibly voice the name of God over and over again, but unless God or the good and the true and the beautiful are viewed as having a validity apart from himself, then his belief is not a dynamic experience, and there is no compelling hand laid upon his will and emotions to do something about it.

Therefore, we are not to judge whether men have a vital religious faith or not by either their professions or their denials. Men are not always aware of what it is they do or do not believe. The acid test is their conduct. "By their fruits ye shall know them."

We can not say we are going to believe such-and-such. Try it and you will see that it just does not work.

No, wherever faith is genuine it seems to be a thing apart from ourselves. Its power is felt within us. It takes place

within us—it functions within us, but we do not possess it—
we are possessed by it. It is not at our beck and call. Like the
wind, it bloweth where it listeth. We can not consciously
bring it into being. We can only await its visitation and then
obey or refuse to obey its promptings.

If we obey, life is filled with meaning and purpose, for
this is the power that creates all values. This is the power that
enables men to hold certain ideal ends as more precious than
their very lives, which arms the crusader for a holy cause with
inexhaustible courage, so that one man is able to chase a
thousand and the voice crying in the wilderness is able to defy
the might of empires. It is the power which impelled a Jesus
to go to the cross and an Albert Schweitzer to give up a successful career at home and proceed to the heart of darkest
Africa to serve a benighted people whom he had never seen
before. It is the "still small voice" which spoke to Elijah on
Mt. Horeb and brought about such a drastic change in his
state of mind.

This is the reality which sends forth the prophet and the
saint to champion well-nigh hopeless ventures, which enables
some men and women at this very moment to strive for peace
among the nations in spite of the almost insurmountable ob-
stacles that seem to be in the way.

Yes, this is the power which sustains us every day of our
lives, even when we are least aware of its presence.

> Men buy and sell by faith: the forges burn,
> The drays are laden, countless mill-wheels turn,
> Great ships are chartered, trains run to and fro;
> Though faith directs them all, they scarcely know
> This spirit of the life of every day.
> Will she desert them when they seek to pray?
>
> A day—a single day—if faith were dead,
> No field were sown, no oven fired for bread.
> Faith is the handmaid in a toiler's guise
> Of all the world of workers. To tired eyes
> With solace she appears at close of day
> To lift their burdens when they seek to pray.[13]

17

Edna St. Vincent Millay underscores the same theme—

> Not Truth, but Faith, it is
> That keeps the world alive. If all at once
> Faith were to slacken—that unconscious Faith
> Which must, I know, yet be the corner stone
> Of all believing—birds now flying fearless
> Across would drop in terror to the earth;
> Fishes would drown; and the all-governing reins
> Would tangle in the frantic hands of God
> And the worlds gallop headlong to destruction! [13a]

If man had not known directly and intimately the power of faith in his own life, the concept of an unseen companion, the idea of a divine guide and counsellor would never have entered his mind. Eliminate this one experience from the human race, and there would have been no such thing as religion. Here is the fact upon which all religions are founded. Here we have isolated the reality which has put the word God into the vocabulary of man.

This God, let me repeat, I identify with the spiritual power within ourselves which idealizes life and then works unceasingly to make real the ideal, which we call Faith when it gives to a possibility the value of a certainty; which we call Hope when it gives to a possibility the value of a probability; and which we call Love when it gives to the potentialities of another person's life the value of present achievement.

In this sense, Faith is something which can not be forced, nor can Hope be forced, and if you will let me distinguish between the love which is a matter of good-will and deliberate affection, on the one hand, and the spontaneous Love which puts a halo around the character of another, which we often describe as blind, but which is one of the most glorious and wondrous experiences in all life, then we may say, neither can Love be forced.

Here is the psychological truth behind Augustine's doctrine of "Grace Bestowed" and Calvin's doctrine of "Divine Election." There are some people who seem to be fortunately blessed with a considerable measure of Faith, Hope and idealizing Love with little effort or merit on their own part, while others seem to be unfortunately vouchsafed a much smaller measure in spite of considerable striving. The former have no cause for self-righteousness, only for humble gratitude. The latter deserve compassion—not condemnation. John Wesley, seeing a convict on his way to the gallows, profoundly observed, "There but for the grace of God, go I." It is always cruel and unjust to persecute or even blame anyone for his lack of Faith, Hope or idealizing Love. These blessings are bestowed by the totality of one's spiritual inheritance, environment and intimations. They are not, let me repeat, at the beck and call of the human will. It was no accident that the apostle Paul summed up the essence of religion by saying, "And now abideth faith, hope and love," [14] for these three powers are essentially one. They together constitute the Great Fact which has given rise to all religions of mankind.

"To have faith is to create. To have hope is to call down blessings. To have love is to work miracles." To have all three is to experience the full presence of Deity.

Go not, my soul, in search of him,
Thou wilt not find him there,
Or in the depths of shadow dim,
Or heights of upper air.
For not in far-off realms of space
The Spirit hath its throne;
In ev'ry heart it findeth place
And waiteth to be known.

Thought answereth alone to thought,
And soul with soul hath kin;
The outward God he findeth not
Who finds not God within
And if the vision come to thee
Revealed by inward sign,
Earth will be full of Deity
And with his glory shine!

Thou shalt not want for company,
Nor pitch thy tent alone;
Th' indwelling God will go with thee,
And show thee of his own.
Then go not thou in search of him,
But to thyself repair;
Wait thou within the silence dim,
And thou shalt find him there! [14a]

CHAPTER 3

THE GOD OF DEVOUT WITNESS

Thus far we have contended that if a God concerned for moral values is to be found at all, He must first be found within the human self. We attempted to show that within man there is a spiritual power that has given rise to his concept of such a Deity—a power that is not subject to the conscious mind to bring into being, and therefore not subject to the control of man's will—a power other than man himself that projects various possibilities on the screen of man's imagination and then impels him to endeavor to turn these possibilities into actualities. We identify this God with the three-fold power of Faith, Hope and idealizing Love, as distinguished on the one hand, from sex-love or, on the other, from man's own capacity for good-will. We maintained that God is not the object of Faith, Hope and Love, but God *is* this Faith, Hope and Love—that the object of this projective process is never a fact, but always a possibility: that Faith gives to a *possibility* of any kind the values of a *certainty;* that Hope gives to a possibility of any kind the value of a probability; and that idealizing Love gives to the potentialities of another's personality the value of a present reality and therefore tends to bring that possibility into being.

We contended further that when Faith, Hope and idealizing Love are real, we do not possess these powers but are possessed by them. We do not use them—they use us as instruments of creation. We came to the conclusion that if man had not known directly and intuitively this marvellous power within his own life, the concept of an unseen companion, the idea of a divine guide and counsellor would never have entered his mind. Eliminate this one experience from the human race and there would have been no such thing as ethical religion.

Here we have isolated the reality which has put the word God into the vocabulary of man. Here is the fact upon which all religions are founded.

That I am not alone in this interpretation of religion, let me cite the opinion of such a distinguished thinker as John Dewey. In his volume entitled *A Common Faith*, he declares:

> A clear and intense conception of a union of ideal ends with actual conditions is capable of arousing steady emotion. . . . Whether one gives the name of "God" to this union operative in thought and action, is a matter of individual decision. But the function of such a working union of the ideal and the actual seems to me identical with the force that has in fact been attached to the conception of God in all the religions; and a clear idea of that function seems to me urgently needed at the present time.[15]

This God is the creative factor in our life which I identify with the process of Faith. This is the reality that Matthew Arnold described as "The Power not ourselves which makes for Righteousness." This is the divine summons that led Abraham to pull up stakes and go into a far country, not knowing whither he went. This is the presence from which Susan B. Anthony could not flee; the same which inspired the Psalmist to sing:

> If I ascend up into heaven, thou art there; if I make my bed in hell, behold thou art there. If I take the wings of the morning and dwell in the uttermost parts of the sea: even there shall thy hand lead me, and thy right hand shall hold me.[16]

This is the creative matrix to which the humanist Dr. E. Burdette Backus is referring when he declares:

> Faith is native to the human heart; it wells up as spontaneously as trees put forth leaves in spring. We have to have faith in order to live; it is one of the essential dy-

namics of our being and it will die only when man ceases to be. We must believe in ourselves, our kind, our ideals, our world. The modern man is under the compulsion of this necessity just as all who have preceded him have been; he, too, has his faith. . . . All that we hold dear—the loves of our homes, our convictions of right and wrong, our quest for the truth, our hopes for the future—are conceived and developed in this matrix. In us the creative forces of the universe are playing another and, to us, supremely important act in the drama of existence; through us new values are coming to birth.[17]

This is the reality which Professor A. N. Whitehead must have had in mind when he wrote in his volume entitled *Science and the Modern World:*

> Religion is the vision of something which stands beyond, behind and within the passing flux of immediate things; something which is real, and yet waiting to be realized; something which is a remote possibility, and yet the greatest of present facts; something that gives meaning to all that passes, and yet eludes apprehension; something whose possession is the final good, and yet is beyond all reach; something which is the ultimate ideal, and the hopeless quest.[18]

This is the experience to which I believe George Bernard Shaw gives devout witness when he declares:

> This is the true joy in life: the being used for a purpose recognized by yourself as a mighty one; the being thoroughly worn out before you are thrown on the scrap heap; the being a force of nature instead of a feverish little clod of ailments and grievances complaining that the world will not devote itself to making you happy.[19]

Just one more quotation to show how God must be identified with the power within man that is constantly impelling him to stretch himself and realize his own potentialities. Here is what Professor C. F. Von Weizsacker, a German philosopher, has to say:

> We must remember that all the gods have human shape. The rationalistic explanation quickly comes to mind that man therefore has made them in his own image. The Bible has it the other way: God created Man in His Image, as His image He created him. This, I believe, is the profounder truth.
>
> In non-mythical terms: the image in which God appears to man does not show what man is but what he might be. It is the image of man's potentiality of being, that which determines his life. This potentiality is for man a power, not a concept. Concepts we have of things past, things we have mastered. But this potentiality is what we have not yet mastered. Man is not master over it. It is master over him. How it happens that the potentiality reveals itself to us, that remains hidden from us. It challenges us, and our life is obedience to it or flight from it. I do not say that this image of the objective potentiality exhausts the idea of divinity. . . . But I believe that this image is the form in which we can best manage to grasp in thought what we know of the divine.[20]

The reality that Professor Weizsacker is talking about makes clear to my mind that much of what is passing for religion today is spurious religion. I refer to the teachings of the cult popularly known as "Peace of Mind" and "Peace of Soul." Here God is portrayed not as a will to be obeyed and served, but as one who serves us and waits upon our desires. But a God who is at man's beck and call is no God at all but a "glorified bell-hop"—a convenient accessory—something which man exploits for his own gratification. However, the testimony of all the great seers and prophets has been that God is a real power in our lives only when we present ourselves to be used by Him for his purposes; not when we try to use Him for our purposes. "Thy will, not mine be done."

24

Therefore, I feel no hesitation in declaring that even the stern majestic Deity preached by the Reverend Jonathan Edwards is a more authentic God than the obliging servant who waits upon man's whims as portrayed by the "Peace of Mind" cults.

The concept of the creative power of Faith, Hope and idealizing Love as the core and center of man's existence is the exact reverse of what many have hitherto looked upon as peripheral and optional. The infinite life within man does not revolve around the finite life within him, but precisely the opposite. Only when the finite finds its center in the infinite— and to the degree it finds this center in the infinite, does "Peace of Mind" come as a natural consequence. Here in my judgment is the psychological truth that moved Augustine to say, "My soul is restless, O God, until it rests in thee."

These two concepts concerning the relation of the finite to the infinite life within man are as antithetical as the Copernican and Ptolemaic theories of the universe. Once we thought that the earth was the center of the universe. It seemed quite obvious that the sun, the moon and the stars pivoted about this earth. The Ptolemaic theory did explain much of the phenomena connected with the changing heavens above. It accounted for the rising and the setting sun and the nightly appearance of the stars. But it did not explain the changing phases of the moon nor adequately account for the eclipses of the sun and many other strange occurrences in the heavens.

The Copernican theory, however, by postulating the sun as the center of a planetary system of which the earth is only one revolving unit among many others, enables us to solve problems which were insoluble on the basis of the previous theory.

By the same token it seems to me that to hold that Faith, Hope and Love pivot about man as a center is to entertain an explanation of spiritual phenomena comparable to the Ptolemaic hypothesis. The only thing to commend it is its apparent plausibility. It, however, does not solve some of the psychological problems which have always perplexed us, such as, for example, man's inability to force his beliefs.

But let man hold that the course of his life is an orbit that swings about Faith, Hope and Love as its spiritual center, then many of his philosophical problems find a satisfactory answer.

We shall merely list what these problems are, without showing their relation to the concept which we have presented, such problems as the seeming indifference of the physical universe to moral values; the paradox of determinism and man's feeling of freedom; the enigma of good and evil side by side; the problem of the one God and the many gods.

It is no wonder that Job was bewildered and perplexed. He was quite confident of an august presence, but when he tried to confront him face to face, he found he could not do so. "Oh that I knew where I might find him," he cried, "that I might come even to his seat. Behold I go forward, but he is not there, and backward, but I can not perceive him." The trouble with Job was that he looked for God in every direction except the one in which he could be found, namely—he failed to recognize the Deity within himself.

Now this discovery is open to every one of us. For men and women in all ages have unwittingly testified to a power within themselves which sometimes lifts them to an exalted plane of living. This power goes with them wherever they go. It expands as their knowledge expands. It can not be overthrown by any blast from the scientific world, for the first duty of science is to bow down before a fact, and this is a real fact. Though intangible, it is the most important fact in the universe, without which there would be no scientific imagination and therefore no science at all.

This God can not be charged with being responsible for the evil in the world, for it is not necessary to attribute either omnipotence or omniscience to him. He is a *struggling Deity* —starting with things as they are and endeavoring to bring order out of chaos; to change the evil into the good, the good into the better, and the better into the best. He is an *experimenting Deity*—constantly trying one method and then another to effect ever higher ends, learning from past failures and building on past achievements.

I am talking not about an abstraction or a mere concept. I am talking about a real presence in the lives of men and women. I am talking about a genuine reality, a fact of human experience, the mystic power of Faith, Hope and of Love, which I identify as the creative power of this universe.

I see this divine creative agency at work in many phases of human endeavor. I see it in a Michelangelo, standing before a block of marble. In his mind's eye an image of majestic form appears, an image more majestic than anything his physical eye has ever seen. At once, his hands are moved to carve that marble block into the likeness of that majestic image and the world is given the sublime statue of Moses.

I see this same wondrous power in a deaf Beethoven sitting before his music sheet. In his mind's ear, he hears wondrous harmonies never before heard on land or sea, and at once he proceeds to make a faithful record so that these harmonies can be reproduced by others long after he himself is dead. And lo, his Fifth Symphony is born.

I see this same divine creative agency at work in the upthrust of social revolution. A young Socialist once said to me, "You may hinder our cause, or you may help it, but you can no more prevent its ultimate triumph than you can prevent the dawning of the morning sun. And why? We are in league with the law of economic determinism." The law of economic determinism, forsooth! Perhaps that law may have no existence except in his own mind, but his faith in it is a dynamic reality to be reckoned with. It is therefore a spiritual power in his life and in the lives of all who share such a belief. It is the creative energy of this universe in a volcanic mood, belching forth hot lava over several countries of this world at this very hour, and shaking the foundations of every institution of human society. The Communist claims to be an Atheist and to be able to leave God entirely out of his calculations, but what kind of a god is he thinking of or are we thinking of, who can be entirely left out of anyone's calculations?

I see this same powerful spiritual force at work in the efforts of responsible statesmen, scientists and religious leaders of this world to avoid the catastrophe of another World War. To them has been vouchsafed the vision of what ought to be and what might be: namely, a world at peace, transformed into a world of incredible abundance, through the constructive rather than the destructive use of the new vast power that is now at the disposal of the human race.

This vision is prodding their minds and imaginations to devise ways and means to bring this potentially blessed state of affairs into being before we all go berserk with fear of one another and use the vast, newly discovered power that has come into our hands for our mutual ruination.

Yes, I see this same sublime originator at work in the Roman Mass. Any concept of Deity that leaves unexplained the amazing persistency of the Roman Catholic Church must be discarded. It is naïve to hold that such an institution which has seen the rise and fall of many empires, has been built upon a foundation of shifting sand. God, to be sure, is not in the consecrated wine and wafer on the altar, unless He was there before the ceremony of consecration; and even so, how could He be known by any first hand experience? But God is nevertheless revealed in the mind of the devout Catholic. By the help of ritual and prayer, his imagination is moved to lean upon an unseen support and lo, underneath are the everlasting arms. The Roman Mass may be theologically unsound, but it is psychologically very profound. Let me remind you it is the psychological approach to the concept of Deity that we are discussing. The devout Catholic, not the nominal Catholic, goes from his church with renewed courage to meet his daily tasks. Though he has been led to look for Deity in a consecrated wafer, he discovers him nevertheless, not in the wine and the wafer, we believe, but where Deity has always been found, namely, within the human soul, where you and I may also find Him if we are persistent enough in our search.

Is this wondrous spiritual power confined merely to man? Has it no existence in the rest of the universe? If such a power does exist in the rest of the universe, how can this fact be known? This will be the subject of the next chapter. In addition, we shall attempt to point out the experience that has given rise to man's concept of the Devil.

CHAPTER 4

THE GOD OF LOGICAL INFERENCE

Since there is a common psychological experience that has
inspired man's concept of God, is there also a common experience that has inspired his concept of the Devil?

I venture to suggest that as Hope, Faith and Love are the
real source of man's idea of a good God, so fear, despair and
hate (as distinguished from anger) are the real source of his
idea of the Devil.

Whenever fear, despair and hate are relevant factors in our
lives, we do not possess them but are possessed by them. Here
we have isolated the psychological experience that has given
rise to the various images of India's Siva, Persia's Ahriman,
Christianity's Satan and Beelzebub, and the numerous demons
of other religions.

Fear, despair and hate have this in common with Hope,
Faith and Love—all are part of the same projective process
within man which we call belief. As Hope gives to a desirable
possibility the value of a probability; and Faith gives to a
desirable possibility the value of a certainty; and creative Love
gives to a desirable possibility in people the value of present
reality, so by the same token fear gives to an undesirable
possibility that threatens us, the value of a probability, and
we are impelled to avoid it; despair gives to an undesirable
possibility the value of a certainty, and we are impelled to
resign ourselves to it. Hate gives to potential evil in people
the value of a present reality and, strangely enough, tends to
bring to pass what it would avoid.

Any realistic appraisal of the spiritual drama that takes
place within the life of man must take account of the destructive as well as constructive forces at work which are just as

29

consistent and no more inconsistent, one with the other, than positive and negative charges of electricity.

All the major religions have been obliged to recognize the wrath of God as well as his love. Some religions have assigned the wrath and love to separate powers, those of God and those of the Devil. But these powers are essentially one—a projective process within man that seeks to bring to pass possibilities that are desirable and to avoid possibilities that are undesirable.

Let me repeat. When Hope, Faith and creative Love on the one hand, and fear, despair and destructive hate on the other are real factors in our lives, we do not possess them but are possessed by them. We are free to resist these spiritual powers, but it always requires an effort on our part to do so. Here is where the doctrine of free will is involved. Both humanists and theists alike recognize this wondrous indwelling power within themselves, the difference between them lying largely in the fact that the theist is able to personify this power and say, "Thou," whereas the humanist feels more sincere in referring to the same reality in less personal terms. This, it seems to me, is the basic difference between these two points of view, all others being mere corollaries and commentaries.

As one who was among the original signers of the Humanist Manifesto, but has since come to see no basic contradiction between humanism and a naturalistic theism that postulates an immanent as over against a supernatural Deity, it has seemed to me that the difference between humanist and theist is largely a matter of vocabulary and not of spiritual reality, surely nothing to get excited about. The fact that humanist and theist can discuss this difference without feeling an impulse to excommunicate each other is indeed something to be grateful for.

To say this is not to overlook the importance of vocabulary as it relates to the religious value of sincerity. To be honest in the use of words is, of course, a common obligation upon theist and humanist alike, and each should respect the efforts of the other to fulfill this obligation, even though the one, in expressing his wonder before the great mystery behind our life, can not go so far as to say, "Thou," while the other

30

can not stop at merely saying "It." Sometimes I find myself saying the one and sometimes the other.

On the religious importance of sincerity, we should all be agreed. However, not all humanists and perhaps not all theists will agree with me from this point on, for from the God within man I am able to postulate the God without.

Is this wondrous spiritual power which man experiences within himself confined merely to him? Has it no existence in the rest of the universe? How can we tell without an inside view of the universe, similar to the one we have of ourselves?

If we cannot see in the whirl of stars and atoms anything more than the interplay of physical forces, perhaps our failure is due to the fact that we have been looking at the universe from the outside, through the telescope, through the microscope, through the spectroscope, when what we need is an entirely new kind of instrument, namely, an "intro-scope" to get an inside view. What could an astronomer, peering at us from some remote star really know about the wondrous mysterious power which is in us? And is not our viewpoint, in relation to the world of nature, even when we look through our most powerful microscopes and telescopes, just as removed and isolated, comparatively speaking, as that of the hypothetical astronomer? Indeed, how can one individual know for certain that even another human being is possessed by this power except as he reads such a meaning into his external behavior? It is an inference—not direct and immediate knowledge. And yet we are able to make this inference every day of our lives, while scarcely realizing it. We have become so skilled in doing so that we take for granted that we know other people when what we know is a mere assumption based on our knowledge of ourselves.

Is it any less reasonable to read such a meaning into the rest of the universe? "If God did not exist," said Voltaire, "it would be necessary to invent Him." [21] God is at least this "intellectual necessity" within man to invent an adequate explanation of the universe. Since we possess no such instrument as an "introscope," to give us an inside view of the universe, may we not logically regard man himself as the best means at hand to give us such a view? Surely man is inside and not outside the evolutionary process. He is a child of this universe. He has been begotten by it. May we not, therefore, reasonably assume that what is explicit in the progeny is at least implicit in the progenitor? May we not logically conclude that the same creative power we experience within ourselves exists also in the animal world from which we have sprung, at least in some degree, and that it must likewise be in the acorn as it pushes miraculously through the sod to lift its arms to the sky? And if in the animal and acorn, why not in the atom and the Milky Way? Many distinguished scientists today have abandoned the mechanistic theory. More and more of them are coming to the conclusion that this universe is charged with dynamic purpose. All creation seems to be moving toward ends and goals. Such a conclusion to be sure is inferential. But so are all our conclusions concerning everything outside ourselves. The whole evolutionary development of our sense organs is nothing more than a colossal experiment in making reliable inferences about the nature of the external world, and so it is from the God within we postulate the God without.

> Were not the eye itself a sun,
>   No sun for it could ever shine;
> By nothing godlike could the heart be won
>   Were not the heart itself divine.[21a]

We digress at this point to show how our sense organs have evolved in response to an external world for this is an essential part of our argument.

The theory of evolution is largely responsible for much of today's religious skepticism. It is being taught in our colleges and universities and taken for granted in our foremost theological seminaries today. There seems to be at this time, in intellectual circles, no question about the fact of evolution. All forms of life on this planet are related, having developed from simpler forms which once wriggled in the primeval ocean. Man, the ape, the tiger, the swordfish, the amoeba, the tree, are cousins to one another; the degree of cousinship being the only matter in dispute. We have been told that the vast development of the various forms of life have come about through the survival of the fittest. The deer, for example, has long legs, not for the purpose of enabling him to escape from his enemies, but because he descended from ancestors who happened to be born with long legs, thus enabling them to escape their enemies, survive, and perpetuate their kind.

Now this mechanical explanation seemed at first thought to rule out any real need or room for a creative power in this universe, and for a while some of the world's greatest thinkers appeared to be entirely satisfied. But sooner or later other leading thinkers and philosophers began to raise pertinent questions.

Yes, the survival of the fittest adequately explains the origin of species, but where did the fittest get their fitness? Whence came the new characteristics and the mutations at birth that gave one offspring the advantage over the other members of his own family? Most of our scientists contend that the mystery of creation still remains a mystery.

Granted the theory of survival of the fittest accounts for the origin of species, but does it account for the origin of the new capacities which differentiate one species from another? It is claimed that they do not. It does not adequately account, for instance, for the emergence of any of our five senses, and especially it does not account for the emergence of the spiritual sense in the human race, namely, the conscience. And do not overlook the fact that conscience is as much a fact as anything we taste, touch, hear, or see. It is part of man's common experience; we cannot throw it out as a fact, whatever theory we must discard in order to account for it. Indeed, some of our scientists look upon the conscience as a rudimentary sixth sense—a spiritual faculty developed within us in response to a spiritual reality existing exterior to ourselves; otherwise there is no natural explanation of its appearance in the life of man.

We have the senses of touch, taste, smell, sight, hearing. How did these come to be? For, of course, there was a time when they did not exist. How then did these various faculties come to be, except in response to an objective reality existing in the universe which made it necessary to take such a reality into account.

For example, the sense of touch has been developed, because there *is* an *objective* world roughly corresponding to our *subjective* world of hot and cold, smooth and rough, soft and hard. The sense of taste has been developed because there is an *objective* world roughly corresponding to our *subjective* world of sour and sweet, bitter and tart, saline and spicy. The sense of smell, likewise, because there was previously an objective world roughly corresponding to our subjective world of foul and fragrant, stale and fresh, rancid and aromatic. And the sense of hearing has been developed because there is an objective world roughly comparable to our subjective world of sound and silence, noise and music, discord and harmony, and the sense of sight because of an objective world roughly corresponding to our subjective world of light and darkness, black and white, and all the colors of the rainbow. And so by the same evolutionary process, it is argued, man has come into possession of his spiritual sense because there is an actual objective world of spiritual reality, which it is absolutely necessary for man to take into account if he would adequately adjust himself to the totality of his environment.

As yet the conscience is but a rudimentary faculty, undeveloped, very uncertain, capable of distinguishing between right and wrong, good and evil, justice and injustice, only in a vague and general way, so that the finer shades of distinction do not obtain for many, while others seem to possess the faculty to a very limited degree. But let us not lose heart, think of the wonderful development that has taken place between the sense of touch in the hoof, say, of a water buffalo, and the sense of touch in the finger of a Helen Keller; between the sense of hearing in a clam and the sense of hearing in a Toscanini; between the moral sense in an Australian bushman and in that of a Jesus or an Albert Schweitzer. Evolution seems to advance in the general direction of a larger and ever larger apprehension of reality and it doth not yet appear what we shall be, for it may yet come to pass that everyone will be able to see spiritual things in clearest outline. "Now we see through a glass darkly," declared the

34

Apostle Paul, "now we know in part, but then shall we know even as also we are known."

What does this mean? Shall God someday be seen? Is this the great reality after which we have been groping so feebly with our moral sense? Is this spiritual faculty now in the process of being developed into a keen and more perfect instrument of discernment until a time may come when it shall be capable of making such accurate discriminations among spiritual things that it will have survival value? Maybe it already has survival value. In fact it may be the only sense, not our five senses, that stands between the human race today and the possibility of its own destruction. If so, there are two courses to follow, we must place less reliance on the negative testimony of those who do not believe and more reliance on the positive testimony of those who do.

Cynics, scoffers, often serve a very useful purpose by keeping the rest of us from making unnecessary fools of ourselves, but theirs is not the type of mind that makes new discoveries or risks new adventures unless the skeptic also has the creative imagination. Now one worm might prove to another that there is no such reality as a world of music and harmony, but we who have listened to a symphony concert know better. One oyster might prove to another that there is no such reality as color and beauty, but we who have been raptured by the rainbow, are entitled to a different opinion. One snail might prove to another that there is no such thing as fragrance and perfume, but we who have inhaled the scent of the rose, or the breath of apple blossoms in the spring are in a superior position to judge. Just so one deficient in the spiritual sense may contend for the non-existence of a world of spiritual reality but those who have actually heard the voice of conscience speaking from within are not likely to deny the reality of spiritual things for very long.

Finally, if this faculty is ever to develop into a more perfect instrument of perception, we must all here and now endeavor to follow its promptings, much more faithfully than hitherto. Just as the rudimentary eye of the flagellata obtained some measure of safety for these minute creatures enabling them to escape from their enemies and propagate their kind, so must we learn to give more obedience to the faintest perceptions of spiritual value. For it may well turn out in the process of evolution that only that race of people will survive to propagate its kind which faithfully follows in the path of moral principles made clear to this inner eye—a race to come which may be as far superior to us in ethical sensitivity as we are to the ape, the tiger and the dinosaur—a race that may even be able to look upon the panorama of the spiritual universe in all its glory. Who knows? The survival of the fittest in the past has always meant the survival of the most faithful. Perhaps after all, the special experiences claimed by Moses, Socrates, Francis of Assisi, and Joan of Arc are not to be explained on the basis of hallucination or self-hypnosis. It could be that the spiritual faculty in them, which seems to be less developed in others, is a form of extra-sensory perception, which suddenly took on new dimensions in them, in response to an exterior reality in the universe, and that what was disclosed to them on rare occasions may someday be the common experience of all the sons of men. At any rate, it seems to my mind now to be entirely within the bounds of reasonable possibility. Whereas once I found it very difficult to believe in a spiritual universe, now I find it difficult not to believe in a spiritual universe.

> O sometimes comes to soul and sense,
> The feeling that is evidence,
> That very near about us lies
> The realm of spirit mysteries.[21b]

Yes, from the presence of the God within ourselves we postulate the God without. We hold that if we possessed an inside view of the universe as we have of ourselves, we might discover the same power at work, shaping and remolding even the world of stars and atoms toward ideal ends. This is something which we shall probably never know directly. We can only infer and trust our inference.

But such an inference is surely the only one that can give adequate meaning to the whole evolutionary development of the spangled heavens above and this terrestrial ball we call our earth and home.

Now, is this mysterious spiritual power personal or impersonal? It depends upon our definition of "personal." If we mean ears, eyes, hands and feet, then, of course, it is not personal. But if we mean a spiritual power known directly, immediately and intimately without the interposition of any of our physical senses, then what could be more personal? It functions within us, does it not? It is a reality closer to us than breathing. To pray is to commune with this infinite spiritual power within man, an act performed by Agnostic, Humanist, Atheist, and Theist alike in varying degrees of rapport whether they be aware of this communion or not; otherwise they could not live. "He that planted the ear, shall he not hear? He that formed the eye, shall he not see?" [22]

> Oh, could we read the Mighty Marvel straight,
> And understand the mystery we are,
> Could we perceive the meaning men call Fate,
> That brought us forth strange children of a star;
> If we could know what word awoke the dead
> Dumb hills, what breath blew on the sea,
> Until a magic turned the stones to bread,
> And the unseeing sought for eyes to see,
> Till living beauty rose up million-winged
> Out of the ashes of a million years,
> And silence broke to music, silver-stringed,
> And sang of Hope and Love and sang of tears,
> Oh we would gather these mute stones and heap
> An altar to that word that woke the deep. [23]

I feel no hesitancy whatsoever in identifying the wondrous mysterious power which we experience within ourselves as that word that woke the deep—the living God, the great original, the tireless creator of new heavens and new earths, whose Sabbath never was nor ever will be, whose life is the light that illuminates the world, whose purposes are revealed to man through various images projected on the screen of his imagination.

37

Someone has suggested that "The mirror of man's mind as a pool must be quiet in order to reflect the image of God." This is the truth Jesus must have referred to when he said, "Blessed are the pure in heart for they shall see God." Since this mirror-pool is probably never perfectly quiet, it can never reflect a perfect image of God. Therefore Jehovah is not God. Allah is not God. Brahma is not God. Jupiter is not God. God is the white light of divinity projected through the defective lens of human personality and then reflected back from the defective screen of human imagination. It is always a distorted image that is reflected. Man therefore does not create God in his own image. It is God who seeks to reveal himself through the imperfect images in man's mind. But only when that image is looked upon as something apart from man's own imagination does it lay compelling hands upon him. To this psychological truth all the great religious seers and prophets have witnessed.

The Burning Bush that set the heart of Moses aflame;

The Seraphim that touched the lips of Isaiah to prophesy;

The Heavenly Dove that descended on Jesus at the time of his baptism;

The Voice that radically altered the purpose of Saul on his way to Damascus;

The Moral Law that filled the mind of Immanuel Kant with awe;

The Love that would not let George Matheson go;

The Truth that lures the philosopher and scientist forever onward;

The Honor that inspires some men to face death rather than do that which is dishonorable—

All these various images have one characteristic in common— they may have had no other existence except in the imagination of those who entertained them, but there they possessed the reality of objectivity. Therefore they were dynamic imperious beliefs which profoundly affected their behavior. God, in short, visits us by enthroning himself on high within the human mind. We ourselves do not enthrone Him but must wait upon His visitation.

If you have found it difficult to follow my thought, you must bear in mind that I am merely in the groping stage of exploring what seems to me to be a fascinating clue to the meaning and purpose of existence.

God is the original ventriloquist. Whenever he speaks authoritatively he seems to speak to us from without, but his is the still small voice that speaks from within.

He is the great magician. He distracts our attention by dreams and visions while he performs his real wonders before our very eyes without our being able to see not only how they are done, but even the one who does them.

He is the indispensable catalyst who brings the real and the ideal together into a workable unity without entering into the combination.

He is the master hypnotist who whispers specific directions to our subconscious minds, and then we go forth to carry them out, offering inadequate conscious explanations for the course we feel compelled to pursue.

He is the understanding psychiatrist behind all psychiatry to whom we turn in private or public confession to help us search our own hearts and straighten out our tangled emotions and conflicting desires.

The majesty of this God is often suddenly revealed to people and in various ways. Sometimes a revelation comes after quiet meditation upon some great truth or under the inspiration of some stimulating personality. Sometimes it comes in hours of solitude; sometimes in the company of a large concourse of people gathered together for an exalted purpose; sometimes in a close call from death or again on the threshold of a challenging opportunity; at other times, when the hush of silence falls upon the house of prayer, or when sublime music stirs us to the depths of our being.

There is no telling when this visitation of Faith and Hope and Love may come, for it can not be forced. But when it comes, a tide of spiritual energy sweeps over us and we are able to do things which seemed utterly impossible before. We

feel lifted up on wings; we are possessed by a sense of wholeness; we are able to face the problems and vicissitudes of life
with more courage and confidence than before.

Whosoever has had such an experience has had an insight
similar to that which has moved many a mystic to declare, "I
have found God and been found by Him," or reverently to
pray—

> Thou life within my life than self more near
> Thou veiled Presence, infinitely clear,
> From all illusive shows of sense I flee
> To find my center and my rest in Thee.[24]

Surely, whosoever has had such an experience can con-
scientiously join in singing at least the humanistic doxology—

> From all that dwells below the skies
> Let faith and hope with love arise,
> Let beauty, truth and good be sung
> In every land and every tongue.[24a]

Perhaps he may also be able to join the Jewish poet, Daniel
Ben Judah, as I am able to do, in exclaiming—

> Praise to the living God!
> All praised be his Name,
> Who was, and is and is to be,
> For aye the same!
> The One Eternal God
> Ere aught that now appears:
> The First, the Last, beyond all thought
> His timeless years![25]

Part II

AFFIRMATION

Chapter 5

ALL MEN PRAY

All men pray whether they are conscious of praying or not. Men have always prayed, and they pray without ceasing. Improbable and impossible as it may at first seem, this universe is so constructed as to make some kind of response to genuine prayer sooner or later.

Making due allowance for heredity and the accidents of fortune, men and women are today what they are, and where they are because of the prayers they prayed in times past, and what they will be tomorrow, and where they will be, is going to be determined largely by their prayers today. For prayer in its fundamental psychological aspects does not depend upon man's conscious belief or disbelief in God. Man prayed before he conceived of any deities. It is as natural for him to pray as to laugh at what is ridiculous, or to cry out in pain. We must get rid of the idea that prayer is primarily a matter of words, of rituals or postures of the body.

As James Montgomery has so aptly defined it in his well known hymn:

> Prayer is the Soul's sincere desire
> Uttered or unexpressed,
> The motion of a hidden fire
> That trembles in the breast.[26]

Prayer in other words is not the idle wish of a moment, a passing whim, a few vocalized phrases directed heavenward, nor an outward ceremony in which one engages either privately or publicly at certain times and places; but rather a deep-seated, sustained longing of the human heart—a persistent yearning of one's deepest self after some end which may or may not be clear to the conscious mind. It is the reaching out of one's whole being after something to which our emotions and imagination have attached a value. It is the secret ambition of one's life to which one unconsciously directs his energies and attention.

To pray is to want something so much that one can scarcely stop thinking about it until he gets it. The difference between people is not that some pray and others do not, but rather in the objects of their prayers and in how honestly, how intelligently, and how earnestly they pray.

An atheist, for example, surely has some sincere desire. The object of his desire may not be the same as that of the Christian, the Jew, or the Mohammedan, but that desire is his prayer.

Men differ greatly in the sincerity with which they pray. Some will address the Deity with a familiarity that betrays an utter lack of reverence. They will readily mouth words that no longer ring true to their real beliefs or to their real experiences. All such are vain repetitions which can do no good.

The first prerequisite of effective prayer is sincerity. Some effort should be made to relate the words of one's mouth to the meditations of one's heart. Many humanists address the Deity in prayer, but the God they have in mind is, of course, not some Deity enthroned on high, but the Divine that is resident in the human heart. Other humanists can not do this without stultification. They prefer to invoke the spirit of truth, beauty and goodness, while still others would use some simpler form of ascription. All are agreed, however, that whatever ascription is used, it should reflect what we really think and what we really feel.

Men differ greatly in the realism with which they pray. There are some things which seem to be outside the province of prayer altogether.

For example, all humanists hold that it is not intelligent to pray for a change in the phenomenon of nature. Most liberal theists also take this same position.

As far as our knowledge goes to date, to petition for sunshine or rain, or to be saved from flood, drouth, earthquake or any other catastrophe of Nature is utterly useless as far as affecting the forces of Nature are concerned.

There seems to be no conclusive evidence to support the belief that human aspirations, desires, or emotions have any influence whatsoever on chemical and physical reactions which take place outside the human body.

Within the human body it is an entirely different story. There is growing evidence that human aspirations, desires and emotions have a great deal to do with people's physical condition.

What about praying for the sick in our hospitals and absent loved ones, who can not hear our prayer, and thus be party to it? Can it do any good? Yes, it can do *us* good, provided *we* do the praying. But we would certainly question whether any change in the physical or spiritual condition of any one can be affected by a supplication in which one does not directly participate, either by making it himself or hearing someone else make it in his behalf.

We refuse to be dogmatic on this point, for if it should some day be demonstrated to the entire satisfaction of the scientific world that there is such a reality as extra-sensory perception, we will gladly recognize it, welcome it, and make use of it. But until that day comes, we believe we have a duty to perform in keeping a critical but open mind on the whole question.

What about praying for a change in our mental and spiritual attitudes? What about praying for things that directly affect our own personal lives and are within the range of possibility? Here we are indeed on more solid ground. This is the chief province of prayer without any question.

Here the persistency of supplication seems to make a difference. If we pray only a little, our prayers are answered only to that degree. If we pray much, we receive a different answer. But whatever our prayer, life sooner or later is bound to make some response. This is what Jesus must have had in mind when he told the story of the man who went to his neighbor at midnight to borrow some bread in order to set before a tired, hungry, and unexpected guest.

The neighbor calls back from an upper window that everybody has gone to bed and it is too much trouble to accommodate him at such an hour. But the man keeps pounding away at his door and pleading so noisily that the neighbor finally gets up in desperation and gives him what he wants. Or, as Jesus puts it:

> Though he will not rise and give him because he is his friend, yet because of his importunity he will rise and give him as much as he needeth. And, I say unto you: Ask and it shall be given you; seek and ye shall find; knock and it shall be opened unto you. For everyone that asketh receiveth; and he that seeketh findeth; and to him that knocketh it shall be opened.[27]

Making due allowance for literary exaggeration, this is fundamentally a true statement about the world in which we live. It is not unwise to hold that prayers are answered, it is unwise to hold that they are not answered. For in the main, the gifts of life are given to those who keep asking for them, the secrets of life are revealed to those who keep searching for them, the doors of life are opened to those who keep knocking at them.

Other things being equal: The universe is on the side of the persistent petitioner and is more than ready to grant his request if it is within the range of possibility.

Ralph Waldo Emerson has said: "Beware what you set your heart upon, for you will surely get it." If this be true, then we should watch how we pray. Before asking, we should consider whether we shall really want what we get after we get it, and before knocking at a door, we should make sure that when it is opened we really desire to pass over the threshold and close it behind us.

The constant prayer of some "is to be at ease, to be discharged from hard and disagreeable tasks, to be called to the solution of no practical problems, to be spared suffering, physical and mental, to have things go on smoothly without

46

much effort." [28] And behold when life responds to their importunity and grants them ease and security and absence of problems, the gifts which they so earnestly sought after turn to ashes in their hands. Now do not think it strange that prayer sometimes brings physical blessings. For when men truly pray, the whole personality goes into action to take advantage of every opportunity that will contribute in any way to the fulfillment of their desire. This is why they should take pains to examine beforehand into the content of their prayers.

Life strangely enough supports "us in our folly as well as in our wisdom, causing the sun to shine and the rain to fall even upon those who are laying up treasures for themselves, even while they grow poor in spirit." [29]

Men and women pray for success, get it, and then discover that their success is a calamity. It had been a thousand times better for them if they had failed.

The story of some of the world's success and the price that is paid for it is a sad and sorrowful tale. Either by their lips or by their actions, which speak louder than words, men signify what they would have for their portion in this world— the thing which beyond all other things they desire and for which they are willing early and late to do their share to help realize. And whether it be wealth, social position, sensual pleasure, ease, quietness, or something else, life does its best to answer these requests wise or foolish, good or harmful, in direct proportion to their intensity.

Many people may pray for power, power over other people, power to control the destiny of others. This is one of the secret prayers of the human spirit. And who gets the power in this world, in the main? Does it necessarily go to our ablest and wisest men? To those who can be trusted to use it justly? "Not often enough."

Bertrand Russell in a recent volume observes:

Where no social condition, such as aristocracy or hereditary monarchy exists to limit the number of men to whom power is possible, those who most desire power, are broadly speaking, those most likely to acquire it . . .

47

Those whose love of power is not strong are unlikely to have much influence on the course of events. The men who cause social changes are as a rule men who strongly desire to do so.[30]

In short, many of today's dictators and rulers, in all probability, would not be where they are unless they had long cherished the thought of power in their inner being and had been willing to pay the price of seeing their prayers fulfilled. I know it may sound almost blasphemous to use the word prayer in such a context, but I believe I am using it in a legitimate sense to describe something real in human experience.

Granted that some object of desire is within the range of physical possibility, I am persuaded that "a man may be and do the thing he wishes, if he keeps that one thought dominant through night and day."

The only trouble is that the thing he wishes may turn out in the end to be the last thing he wants when he gets it.

How important then to combine intelligence with desire, to add wisdom to our petitions—to show discrimination in our longings and questings—in short, to learn from the experience of the past, what the worthwhile things in life are for which we should pray. Now this is exactly the purpose of public worship, viz., to purify, to edify, to modify the sincere desire of human hearts so that we shall not be disappointed and harmed when our prayers are granted.

Religion with wisdom born of centuries of experience tells us that qualities of mind and heart, rather than physical blessings, should be our major concern. We should pray not for more of the bounties of life, but for a greater sense of gratitude, not for more excitement and sensation, but for more awareness of life, not for more recognition and love from our fellowmen, but for more capacity to give love and recognition, not to be delivered from temptation, not to be saved from sorrow and suffering, but to be able to endure both without being overcome by either, not to be spared disappointment, defeat and frustration, but to be possessed

48

of the courage to rise again and face the challenge of the morrow.

These are some of the things which are truly worth praying for, which will not turn to ashes in our hands when we get them, and they are all within the range of possibility for every one of us.

This chapter has been concerned with only one aspect of prayer, namely, prayer as petition. Of course there are other aspects which are equally important, such as thanksgiving, confession, and resignation, all open to a perfectly natural explanation without the necessity of believing in anything supernatural.

The point to be stressed is the creative power of faith when it takes the form of petition. If one's petition is sustained, changes take place either within one's self or without, which otherwise would not occur. Here is a vital experience common to all men whether they are fully aware of it or not, whether they call themselves theists, atheists, humanists, agnostics, skeptics or something else.

There is always some answer to the soul's sincere desire and related to that desire even if it is not the answer for which we hoped.

CHAPTER 6

MIRACLES MEASURE OUR IGNORANCE OF UNIVERSAL LAWS

Most of the religions of mankind are supported by numerous tales of signs and wonders alleged to have been performed by their respective seers and prophets. The religion which is most free of such tales is undoubtedly Confucianism. Confucius himself was such a rational, matter-of-fact personality that it has been very difficult to clutter up his reputation with myth and miracle although many attempts have been made to do so.

Among the religions which have placed great credence in accounts of the miraculous we must list the Jewish-Christian faith. Hinduism is probably the most heavily laden with incredible tales, but Christianity is not far behind. Both the Old Testament and the New Testament are full of such stories, all the way from Aaron who is alleged to have twisted a wooden rod into a coiling serpent before the eyes of the Pharaoh to the Apostle Paul who is reported to have healed the halt and the blind by the laying on of hands. In the gospel accounts there are thirty-five miracles attributed to Jesus of Nazareth alone, including several alleged examples of his power to control the forces of nature.

To most religious liberals all such tales greatly detract from, rather than add to, our confidence in the Bible as an authentic repository of truth and history. President Thomas Jefferson was so repelled by them that he composed a *Life of Jesus* in which all stories of the supernatural were eliminated. It is called the Jefferson Bible. One has only to glance through it to realize how little of the beauty and inspiration of the Gospel story is lost when no mention of the miraculous is made. And yet millions look upon the Bible of Christianity as the very word of God himself, partly if not largely because it does contain these very tales of marvel and mystery.

What then should be the attitude of religious liberals toward this question? First of all it is necessary for us to define our terms. What do we mean by the word miraculous. If we mean something taking place in the physical world *contrary to all the laws of nature,* then most religious liberals do not believe in miracles. On the contrary, we believe in the universal reign of law. We hold that nothing takes place in this universe without an adequate cause. Our attitude toward miracles is vitally and logically related to our concept of Deity. We have given up belief in a supernatural God and we have therefore given up belief in supernatural intervention in the life of the world. Whenever anything takes place out of the ordinary, we look for a natural explanation. If, however, we mean by "miracle" an event or effect in the physical world deviating from the known laws of nature or transcending our knowledge of those laws, then of course religious liberals are obliged to recognize that there are such realities as miracles. Many of the discoveries of science have come about because someone took notice of deviations from what was held to be the known laws of nature.

The word "miracle" comes from a Latin verb meaning to wonder. Well, there are many things in this universe which we do not fully understand, and if we possess any imagination at all we are compelled to wonder. To wonder is to be curious about something that is beyond our present knowledge and ordinary experience. An electric light seen for the first time by some Hottentot would be a miracle to him. Its illumination would transcend his knowledge of the laws of nature. And in the same manner the capacity of today's radio to capture music from the ether is still pretty much of a miracle, especially to those of us who have only a vague idea of what actually takes place, although we have long since learned to accept the radio as a part of everyday experience.

The word "miracle" therefore is a relative term. In a very real sense it is really a measure of our lack of knowledge in any given instance. What may be regarded as a miracle

51

by one person or by one age may not be regarded as a miracle by another person or another age. The great miracle, the wonder of wonders, the supreme marvel, is the fact of life itself. All the rest is child's play in comparison.

However, there still remains the question—What shall be our attitude toward the tales of wonder in the Bible? Is it necessary to reject them all because we cannot believe in some of them? Or is it possible to believe in some of them while rejecting others? To answer this question we must first understand the age in which the Bible was composed. The Bible was written over a period of one thousand years, and that period was an age of easy credulity. It was an age that knew little about the laws of physics, chemistry, astronomy, or physical health—the keeping of scientific records and the method of historical research were largely unknown. If in this age thousands of people can believe that a wooden or stone image of the Virgin will shed tears, what must the people in an unscientific age have been able to believe? It would have been a miracle indeed if all tales of the miraculous had been kept out of such a book as the Bible.

Some of the tales religious liberals reject are utterly incredible—such as Moses causing the Red Sea to roll back at the sound of his voice—or Joshua commanding the sun to stand still—or Jesus walking on the sea, stilling the waves of the tempest by word of mouth—or turning water into wine.

Of course it is not necessary to take the position that all these stories were made out of whole cloth, for possibly in each case something real enough may very well have happened, but what we cannot accept is the inadequate explanation which is offered. For instance, when the children of Israel pressed forward to the narrow arm of the Red Sea which extends far into the land of Goshen there may have been a timely ebbing of the tide which runs pretty high in that particular region, and then a fortunate returning of the tide by the time the pursuing Egyptians had reached its shore. The use of the word fortunate depends, of course, upon whether one is looking from the Hebrew or the Egyptian point-of-view. In neither case can we believe that the command of Moses had anything to do with the behavior of the sea. It was simply "a lucky break" for the Israelites, as we would say in the idiom of the street, and by the same token "an unlucky break" for the Egyptians. The flight from Egypt took place long before the Israelites had the tools to preserve the story in writing. We do not know even the century, let alone the year, in which the flight took place.

Plausible explanations of the nature miracles to be found in the Bible have been offered by devout scholars in nearly every instance. Some of them are quite fascinating in their ingenuity. But we would not falter in our faith in nature's laws, even if no plausible explanation were forthcoming. We would be more anxious to save the reputation of nature for trustworthiness than the reputation of any witness to her wonders.

Let us now turn to some of the other miracles. In the Gospel accounts of Jesus there are three instances where he is alleged to have raised the dead to life, but in each case Jesus himself avoided making any such claim.

In the case of the daughter of Jairus, Jesus says very definitely, "The maid is not dead but sleepeth." In the case of Lazarus, he says, "This sickness is not unto death," and again later on "Our friend Lazarus sleepeth, but I go that I may awake him out of sleep." In the case of the widow's son who was being carried away on a bier, Jesus went up to his side and said, "Young man, I say unto thee arise," and then the writer goes on to add his own opinion of what took place—"and he that was dead sat up and began to speak." In this case we are not told whether Jesus himself believed the man was merely sleeping, as in the other two instances, or was really dead. We have only the testimony of a witness who was incompetent to judge for there was no physician present. But suppose there had been! The physicians of the first century did not possess the scientific means to determine the signs of death beyond the peradventure of a doubt. Even modern physicians, with the best of equipment, sometimes make mistakes in such matters.

We see no reason to doubt the reality of what happened to the widow's son when Jesus commanded him to arise.

What we doubt is the accuracy of the diagnosis of his previous condition. There have been numerous modern authenticated cases of sudden resuscitations of life in those who were thought to be dead, but we would not think of classing any of them as miracles even in the broad sense of the dictionary's definition of that term. So much for the tales of the dead raised to life.

Next let us consider the many stories in the Bible about faith cures—such for example as the healing of Peter's mother-in-law who was sick with fever; the giving of sight to the blind and hearing to the deaf, and speech to the dumb, and restoration to the lame and the halt, the palsied and the paralytic. What position do religious liberals take in regard to these scriptural accounts of healing marvel? Well, fifty or sixty years ago probably most liberals would have rejected them as incredible tales. Surely many would have raised their eyebrows at the suggestion that they should be taken seriously. But today there is a different attitude.

We know now that within the past two generations considerable research has been made in the field of human psychology. Hypnotism which was once rejected as a fraud is now accepted as a fact in scientific circles. The uses of auto-suggestion have been explored and exploited with no little success. Great strides have been made in the art of psycho-analysis, and the trained psychiatrist is today an accredited addition to the healing profession. We understand now that there is a vital relation between mental health and physical health; that mental sickness is a frequent cause of bodily illness, and vice versa. Many of us in recent years, from the vantage point of today's experiments in psycho-therapy, have been changing our minds about some of the miracles attributed to Jesus.

We can well believe now that Jesus of Nazareth, with his captivating, magnetic personality could have brought about startling physical changes in the lives of those who early sought healing at his hands by the use of psychological means alone. Repressed feelings of guilt, hidden fears and obsessions, deep-seated wounds and resentments can sometimes neutralize

54

the good effects of all the medicine in the world, and all the fresh air and nourishing food as well.

The age in which Jesus lived had its full share of diseases of the body due to diseases of the mind. It was an age in which rumors of the wonder worker lost none of their wonder in the telling. Such rumors spread like wild fire. The people were anxious to believe what was in line with their needs; trained physicians were scarce. The best of them did not have a high rating in successful cures. Here was someone quite out of the ordinary, who spoke as one having authority, whose voice sounded the note of confidence and assurance. The people were electric with the eagerness of expectancy. A word from his lips or a touch from his hand, or even a glance from his eye, was enough to bring it to a high voltage point. The people crowded around Jesus, not so much to hear him speak but to see what he could do.

There is much evidence to show that Jesus was anxious to avoid getting a reputation as a wonder-worker. He believed it was going to hinder his real mission more than to help it. When the Scribes and Pharisees came to him asking for a sign of his prophethood, he replied: "An evil and adulterous age seeketh after a sign, but no sign shall be given except the sign of the prophet Jonah," namely, a clarion call to repentance. But the role of wonder-worker was thrust upon Jesus by the clamoring of the general public who insisted upon bringing their sick and ailing loved ones to his attention, and he was too much filled with pity to turn them aside altogether. How often Jesus said to those who claimed a cure at his hands— "Son, daughter, thy faith hath made thee whole." [31] "Go thy way and tell no man of it," as if he was anxious to keep this part of his work as quiet as possible.

It is not necessary, therefore, to attribute supernatural power to Jesus to account for any one of the numerous faith cures attributed to him. Modern psychotherapy has been able to duplicate the major portion of them under clinical auspices. Dr. George B. Cutten, Ex-President of Colgate University, makes this clear-cut statement in his volume on *Psychological Phenomena of Christianity*: "Of the forty miracles performed by Jesus and the Apostles on the bodies of men all classes but three have been duplicated by hypnotism." [32]

It is interesting in this connection to note that all the miracles described in the Gospel of John are of the incredible sort. There are seven of them in number, and only one is common to the other Gospels. The Gospel of John was written anywhere from ninety to one hundred and twenty-five years after the events described. Nearly all the faith cures common to the other gospels have been duplicated by the modern psychiatrist. Steady progress is being made in this kind of healing every year. The future is bright with the prospect of even greater things to come. As yet we are only in the kindergarten stage of understanding the mystery of the human mind, or the nature of the universe. Scientific research is probing into many dark corners of the unknown. It is only a little more than a decade since the secret of atomic power was successfully unlocked for the first time.

A thousand and one experiments of vast importance to the future welfare of mankind are undoubtedly being carried out at the present hour which will further lift the veil of mystery that surrounds our life on this planet. Some day a comparatively inexpensive way to change sea water into fresh water will be announced to the world. Think what that would mean! Eventually the deserts will be made to blossom as the rose.

The age of miracles is by no means confined to the distant past. The age of greater miracles is already upon us.

Wonders still the world shall witness
Never known by men of old,
Never dreamed by ancient sages,
Howsoever free and bold.
Sons and daughters shall inherit
Wondrous arts to us unknown
When the dawn of Peace its splendor
Over all the world has thrown. [33]

Yes, the age of greater miracles than the world has ever known before awaits the lifting of the terrible burden of war

56

and the release of human effort for the constructive ends of peace. Then indeed shall we behold many mighty works, and the spirit of man shall look out upon the universe and truly marvel at its signs and wonders. But it will not be necessary to hold that any of these signs and wonders are contrary to the laws of nature.

CHAPTER 7

MOST RITES AND CEREMONIES SERVE SOME TRUTH

What should be our attitude toward ceremonies and the ceremonial observance of holy days?

At the outset I want to make clear that when I use the expression "Holy Days" I am employing a figure of speech, the figure of personification, for, of course, holiness does not pertain to times and occasions but only to persons and motivations. One day is no more holy in itself than another day. It is our motive and purpose in observing it that makes it holy or not.

On this question of ceremonies and holy days, as on most other questions it is only fair to state that there is a wide diversity of conviction. For example—there are those who are very much bored by all ceremonies and ceremonial observances. Some have left the church of their childhood to get as far away as possible from all such practices. Rites and rituals as a rule leave them cold and inattentive. They are inclined to look upon the forms and formalities of public worship as the sounding brass and clanging cymbals of religion, or as so much chaff which the wind driveth away. They certainly do not constitute the kernel of inspiration they hope to get out of a service of worship. What they go to church for is the *sermon*—a serious discussion of religious principles and their practical application to every day affairs —and this regardless who the preacher is. So they are inclined to avoid what they are pleased to look upon as the preliminaries. They do not consider that they have missed very much that is important in a service of worship, provided they have arrived in time for the sermon. Now there are many liberals who hold this point of view and their number includes not a few of our most respected people.

58

On the other hand there are those who are very much interested in rites and ceremonies. What they would like to see in our churches is a much more ornate service of worship. They are inclined to believe that we have made altogether too much of a fetish of the sermon and not enough of the inspirational value of ritualistic forms. These would like to see more colorful vestments of all kinds—more pageantry and more dramatic presentations of religious truths and more generous use of religious symbols. This point of view is not confined alone to the theists for there are humanists who are just as much interested in rites and ceremonies as any theist ever thought of being. In fact it is the humanists who are offering most of the present new material for enhancing the beauty of our services of worship.

The cleavage between humanism and theism has nothing to do with the question of rites and ceremonies. There is probably just as large a percentage of theists as humanists who are bored by them, and just as large a percentage of humanists as theists who are vitally concerned with them. In between these two extremes there are liberals who manifest varying degrees of indifference and interest.

On one point, however, we are all agreed. We are all agreed that there is no rite or ceremony to which we are ready to ascribe the value of a *sacrament*. We are all agreed that nothing magical or supernatural takes place when we baptize our children, ordain our ministers, or perform the marriage ceremony, or conduct the last rites for our dead.

We can not believe that any priest or minister can say a few words over ordinary wine and bread and change that wine and bread into the blood and body of Deity, the consumption of which automatically assures immortality. No, that is too easy a way to be saved. It is incantation and does not differ essentially from the mumbo-jumbo of the ancient medicine man.

For the same reason we cannot believe that the water used in a baptismal service is any different from the water we use in washing our garments. It is not charged with some unseen, hidden quality that enters into it on being blessed. It does not perform any magical effect.

We cannot believe that a preacher, who has had some one else lay his hands on him, possesses any more ethical or spiritual authority to preach than he had before. There is no mysterious power that is transferred by the mere laying on of hands.

We cannot believe that anything we say or do at the funeral service of any person can affect one way or the other the future welfare of that person in whatever life may obtain beyond the grave. The usefulness of all these rites and ceremonies lies wholly in their symbolic value. Unless they remind us of our spiritual duties and responsibilities they are without any value in themselves. They are means to ends. When we look upon them as *ends* then they become stumbling blocks and hindrances,—not aids to a vital religious experience.

It is a well established fact that the greatest religious prophets have been lined up on the side opposed to empty rites and ceremonies. From the earliest time they have pointed out the peril of smothering the spiritual life of man by a multitude of ritualistic forms and observances. Eight centuries before Jesus the Prophet Amos was among the first to expose this peril, for he makes the God of Israel to say, "Take away from me the noise of thy songs for I will not hear the melody of thy viols. But let justice roll down as waters and righteousness as any overflowing stream . . . then shall the Lord of Hosts be gracious unto you and hear you." [33a]

In a famous passage the Prophet Isaiah makes the God of Israel to say, "Bring no more vain oblations. Incense is an abomination unto me; the new moons and sabbaths, the calling of assemblies, I cannot away with; it is iniquity, even the solemn meeting. Your new moons and your appointed feasts my soul hateth; they are a trouble unto me; I am weary to bear them. And when ye spread forth your hands, I will hide mine eyes from you; yea, when ye make prayers, I will not hear: your hands are full of blood." [33b] And so on with much more in a similar vein.

Micah was another prophet to point out the peril and emptiness of mere ritual. "Wherewith shall I come before the Lord and bow myself before the High God? Shall I come before him with burnt offerings, with calves a year old? Will the Lord be pleased with thousands of rams or with ten thousands of rivers of oil? ... He hath shewed thee, O man, what is good. And what doth the Lord require of thee but to do justly, to love mercy, and to walk humbly with thy God." [33c]

Jesus of Nazareth took essentially the same point of view when he condemned the church people of his day for paying too much attention to the outward forms of religion. He rebuked the Scribes and Pharisees for making long prayers in public and using vain repetitions and mummery as a substitute for moral conduct. Quoting one of the Hebrew prophets, he declared, "This people honoreth me with their lips, but their heart is far from me. Howbeit, in vain do they worship me, teaching for doctrines the commandments of man." [34]

Strange, is it not, that a religious teacher who exhibited so little interest in producing forms of worship as Jesus did should have inspired a religion which later on created the most ornate rites and ceremonies in the whole history of religion!

Why then do we have rites and the ceremonial observance of holy days? The answer is quite obvious. Because we cannot help ourselves. Even Jesus could not avoid ceremonies altogether, as evidenced by the fact that he submitted to baptism at the hands of John, observed the Passover Feast, ceremoniously washed the feet of his disciples, and rode on a donkey to dramatize his entry into Jerusalem, with the pageantry of palm branches and the singing of psalms. He said to those who would rebuke his disciples for this unrestrained demonstration—"If the mouths of these people were stopped even the stones would break forth into singing." Man has rites and ceremonies because he cannot help himself. It is because man often has something to express which he can express in no other way. He has deep-seated feelings which he cannot communicate except in the language of symbolism and ritual. It is his natural instinct for poetry that inspires him to create *new* rites and ceremonies even while he is denouncing and discarding the *old*.

Even those who deny their interest in all rites and ceremonies are ready enough to shake hands with their friends and acquaintances on meeting them, and thus they participate in one of the oldest and most satisfying of all ceremonies, for the practice of shaking hands is merely a ceremony which has so long been observed that we no longer think of it as such. It is only necessary to visit some country where the shaking of hands is not the practice on greeting friends to realize its ceremonial nature. Tipping one's hat to a woman on the street, or holding her chair at the dinner table, are ritualistic acts so old that we look upon them merely as customs.

When we hold a birthday party and bring in the cake with its lighted candles we are really performing a ceremony. Why go to all the trouble of putting lighted candles on a cake and then deliberately blowing them out soon after? Because it adds to the beauty and merriment of the occasion.

To make a ceremony of anything means to do something extra—which we could get along without doing, of course, but which if added enhances its value for us beyond its cost in time and energy.

Why do we take such pains to color eggs for the coming of Easter? They are not going to taste any better. It is because the colored egg has been long associated with the gladness of springtime, and we find considerable pleasure in this simple ritual.

Why do we take such pains at Christmas or Hanukka to wrap up our gifts? Because we obtain considerable pleasure by the simple ceremony of wrapping and unwrapping them.

Every year many of our boys and girls participate in commencement exercises in schools, colleges and universities. We probably could get along without these ceremonies—sometimes they are very boring indeed. But I think you will agree that when they are carried out beautifully they can be made most inspiring.

How poor all our lives would be—how drab and barren—if there were no rites and ceremonies of any kind! No wedding ritual, no birthday celebrations, no inauguration exercises, no official laying of corner-stones for schools and libraries and other public buildings, no Thanksgiving rites, no Christmas celebration, no Passover or Easter pageantry, no Hallowe'en ritual to observe, no sending of flowers to the sick as a symbol of love and affection, no clasping of hands as a sign of respect and friendliness!

Why do we have rites and ceremonial observances of certain important days in the year? Because we like them when they have meaning and content for us. They add poetry to the prose of man's existence on this planet. They help us to prolong the savor of present joys and enthusiasms. They serve to recapture for us the reverent or festive moods of former days and occasions. They help us to fix in our memories important events which can not be too often recalled. They serve to dignify the inevitable tragedies of our common life. They are useful in dramatizing our inescapable duties and responsibilities. They enable us to express in outward form some of the deepest emotions of the human spirit which could not otherwise find adequate expression. They enable us to communicate the values and aspirations which one generation cherishes to those coming after.

No, what most people really oppose are not rites and ceremonies in themselves, but rites and ceremonies which have lost their inspirational value—which no longer have any present meaning and content, or have a meaning and content to which they can no longer sincerely subscribe.

It is no easy task which a rabbi of a synagogue or a minister of a church confronts today. His is the responsibility of conducting regular services of worship for a congregation who have widely differing intellectual attitudes and aesthetic tastes. He cannot hope to meet the spiritual needs or express the aspirations of every one in every service of worship. The most he can reasonably expect to achieve is to provide forms of worship which express the religious aspirations of most *some* of the time, without doing too much violence to the deep-seated convictions of anyone at any time. At no time, however, can he afford to particpate in any ritual which is not sincerely endorsed by himself, for in this direction lies spiritual stultificaton for both the congregation and himself.

There is one day in the religious calendar of holy days in whose ceremonial observance we can participate with unbounded enthusiasm, and without reservations of any kind. Palm Sunday is surely such a holy day—the farthest removed from all suggestion of sham or superstition or dubious dogma. It celebrates one of the sublime events in the annals of human heroism. It marks the turning point in the career of Jesus when he fared forth with nothing but his courage and idealism to defy the entrenched forces of political and ecclesiastical power, and to capture the capital city of his people in the name and in the spirit of truth and righteousness. Even though his triumph was but for a day, and though frustration and crucifixion followed swiftly in its train, nevertheless the sheer audacity of his example and the complete unselfishness of his motives have inspired many a generation of youth ever since to go forth with the same high purpose to remold the world a little nearer to the heart's desire. When we pause to consider the grandeur of his personality, we too cannot help but be stirred with sublime emotions and high resolutions as were the throngs two thousand years ago, and be moved to sing hosannas to his name.

Hanukka or the Jewish Feast of Lights is certainly another ceremonial occasion that can be observed with enthusiasm and without reservations of any kind by Christians as well as Jews. For Hanukka also celebrates one of the sublime events in the annals of human heroism. A handful of desperate people made desperate by the terrible exactions of a cruel tyranny gathered together under the leadership of Judas Maccabeus, and with their backs to the wall and against over-whelming odds courageously and triumphantly threw off the yoke of foreign bondage. Here we have a sublime example of the tremendous power of conscience and conviction, when right actually made for might and much inspiration can come from reverently recalling this historic event.

The celebration of Christmas, however, presents difficulties for many people because of the myths and legends concerning the birth of Jesus which they no longer can or never could accept as authentic history. They understand that similar tales of wonder have been told about the birth of several other founders of religion, no less incredible if taken literally. But once these myths and legends are frankly regarded as the poetry of an authentic experience and a serious attempt is made to discover the truth behind the poetry, one may be richly rewarded with an authentic religious experience of his own. Here is what I see in these tales of wonder.

The Christmas story dramatizes a profound truth. It dramatizes man's recognition of the pre-eminence of virtue—the Divinity of goodness.

Consider how the human fancy has again and again glorified the lives of its tribal war lords, its Goliaths, its conquering kings and imperious Caesars.

How often it has held up for the emulation of the world the man of mere brute strength, of blood and iron, of unscrupulous power, of selfish ambition or of ruthless greed!

But here in the Christmas story we have a glorification of an entirely different order. Here we have the glorification of mercy and goodness and all that is best in human nature.

Behold a man of peace becomes the hero of heroes; one who ministered unto others becomes the king of kings; a meek and lowly one becomes the lord of lords. And the religious imagination is impelled to give his birth a cosmic setting.

What a strange phenomenon is this! How incredible! What a contrast to the belligerent instincts of Simian and Savage! It speaks volumes about the ethical evolution of man, does it not? If millions of people can respond with enthusiasm to the sublime character of Jesus, surely it is because their own minds and hearts are charged with Divinity. If they would clothe Him with the power and majesty of God, it shows the moral stuff of which they are made.

The fact that in other lands and climes such high-minded men as Gautama, Confucius and Laotze have been similarly deified shows how universal is this urge to exalt goodness. In India today the exaltation of the saintly Gandhi is already well under way.

It is significant that goodness can co-exist with evil but it is even more significant that man has reserved his highest and most enduring veneration for those who had faith in

65

the power of goodness to overcome evil in the end and proved their faith by their lives.

Therefore the sacred light which streams from the Star of Bethlehem is the light which it throws upon the potential God-likeness of human nature, which in turn throws light upon the ultimate nature of the universe itself.

This is the secret of the Christmas radiance. It is the Divine Splendor breaking through the human soul, inspiring it to rejoice with exceeding great joy.

Yes, behind most rites and ceremonies there is some important truth. It is worthwhile to look for that truth before rejecting any as completely superstitious. For there can be superstition in avoiding superstition.

CHAPTER 8

HOW WE WORK REVEALS OUR WORSHIP

Anxious and responsible leaders of organized religion have been recently deploring the rise of secularism in our midst, and a corresponding decline in the practice of religious worship as it once prevailed in this country. President Pusey of Harvard University had an article not long ago in *The Christian Century* on this very subject entitled "The Relation of Secularism and Religion." Now it is true that more people, even percentage-wise, are attending churches today than ever before in the history of our country and are becoming members; but at the same time it is true that many of the accustomed forms of worship are being dropped. For example, fewer and fewer homes percentage-wise are saying grace before meals. The old family altar, morning and evening, has gone out of fashion. The sick and the dying are calling less frequently upon the ministrations of the clergy. When they are ill they inform their doctors by telephone and their ministers by telepathy. Only in the formal church service does the practice of prayer, for example, prevail as formerly, but even here it is tolerated more as a time-honored custom than as an indispensable spiritual need.

Now does this apparent decline in the use of accustomed forms of worship mean that the spirit of true worship is also declining in our midst? I for one do not believe this is necessarily so. In my judgment the spirit of worship is not dying out and cannot die out but is merely expressing itself in ways and modes more characteristic of the age in which we live.

Forms of worship may come and go, but the spirit of worship goes on forever. Man's reverence before the great mystery of life will probably always remain. The rituals of expressing this reverence do change, however, from age to age. For example, there was a time when reverence before th great mystery of life was shown by man's readiness to sacrifice his first-born child to the gods, and the parent unwilling to make such a sacrifice was considered irreligious. A huge step forward was made when animals were substituted for human sacrifice. People wondered what was going to become of religion. Well, the spirit of worship did not die out because of this shocking change.

And still another step forward was made when sweet smelling incense and the music of stringed instruments were substituted for the slaughter of beasts. True worship did not decline on that account.

Then the prophets of righteousness, the great Hebrew prophets—began to cry out in the name of God, "Bring no more vain oblations, incense is an abomination unto me, the new moons and sabbaths, the calling of assemblies, I cannot away with; it is iniquity, even the solemn meeting. . . . Wash you; make you clean." [35] Another great Hebrew prophet declared, "What doth the Lord require of thee, but to do justly and to love mercy and to walk humbly with thy God." [36] Holy righteous conduct as a means of showing one's reverence for the great mystery of life was in truth the mightiest step forward in the entire development of man's ritual of worship. The ecclesiastical world has yet to reach the high standards set before them by these great prophets of the sixth and seventh centuries before Christ. But even thus far the ritual of righteous behavior has resulted in a progressively more vital and wholesome worship for the great masses of mankind.

We are now in the midst of another significant religious change in this matter of worship due to our better understanding of the nature of the universe in which we live. It is not so much a step forward as a leap forward, a leap forward in imagination. The enlightened world is pretty much agreed, that whatever may be said about the wondrous life behind our own whether personified or otherwise regarded, we cannot believe that He is a mere sensualist, who delights in incense and incantations. Neither can we believe that He is an egoist, who covets flattery and praise, nor that He is merely a cosmic humanitarian, primarily interested in generous and unselfish conduct, good as that is. It is coming to be seen that the ultimate reality behind our universe is a creative power. God whether personified or not is a tireless toiler, a worker, an artisan, yes, an artist, if you please, who hates inactivity and laziness, to whom bunglesome workmanship is utter abomination. Call this reality by whatever name you choose, He seems to be primarily interested in bringing things to pass that never before existed. "Lightning and light, wind and wave, frost and flame, and all the secret subtle powers of earth and air," [37] are his tireless toilers. This is the kind of God that is being revealed to us by modern science, and philosophy.

Now if this be true, and I believe it to be true, then this kind of God can only be worshipped by the ritual of creative effort, by the holiness of toil, by the sacredness of sweat. Whether the sweat be of body, of mind, or of soul, or whether the toil be of hand or brain, or both, it makes but little difference; the worship is all the same, and we believe acceptable to the kind of God that now seems to be revealed to us.

Twenty-three centuries ago this concept of work as worship was anticipated by the author of Ecclesiasticus when he praised the artisan and the artist declaring, "For these maintain the fabric of the world, and in the handiwork of their craft is their prayer." And many of us believe that those words of Jesus express the same idea, the lost sayings that were found at Oxyrhynchus in Egypt. "Jesus saith, Wherever there are two, they are not without God; and wherever there is one alone, I say, I am with him. Raise the stone and there shalt thou find me; cleave the wood and there am I." [38] Apparently the quarryman in raising the stone, the woodsman in cleaving the wood are taking a significant part in worshipping the wonder of this universe. Emerson said the same thing when he declared, "A man's work is his sincerest prayer." Thomas Carlyle, of course, is the great champion of this point of view. He proclaims that all true work is sacred. "Labor wide as the earth has its summit in the heavens. The sweat of the brow, and up from that the sweat of the brain and sweat of the heart. . . . O brother if this universe is its unceasing creativity, and if work is the noblest thing yet discovered under God's sky!" [39]

Now if this be true, if the most significant thing about this universe is its unceasing creativity, and if work is the sincerest prayer, let us consider the various kinds of worshippers in our midst and analyze the prayers they are praying by their deeds, regardless of the posture of their bodies.

In my judgment there is first of all the prayer of the frustrated, namely, the unemployed. What kind of a prayer do they pray? Incredible as it may seem to some of us, there are thousands of able bodied men in this country at this very moment who want work and cannot find it. Even in our most prosperous years, we always seem to have an army of unemployed honestly seeking employment. Economists are predicting that if peace should break out and some general program of disarmament should be adopted, it would be immediately followed, without a doubt, by a period of economic adjustment, which could possibly throw more millions of people out of work than the depression of the early thirties. The economic tragedy, of course, would be bad enough, but the spiritual tragedy would, in my judgment, be even worse. In a universe that apparently abhors inactivity, there are always people, especially in our highly industrialized centers, condemned periodically by force of circumstances to give up a portion of their right to worship fully; for without work they cannot express completely their basic spiritual aspirations. For men and women must be engaged in useful labor, not merely to achieve a livelihood, but also to achieve a life of meaning and purpose. Therefore, those who are condemned to enforced idleness, at any time and for whatever reason, deserve our deepest sympathy, for theirs is indeed a prayer of desperation. With outstretched arms they cry, "O wretched man that I am who shall deliver me from the body of this death?" [40] We must find some more satisfactory answer to this problem than we have found to date.

Secondly, there is the prayer of the restless dilettantes.

70

There are those who always dislike what they are actually doing in this world because they think they are fitted for something else, which they have not tried as yet, but which they think they would like much better. As a result they flit from task to task without getting any joy or satisfaction out of any. They are like the worshippers who visit many churches but never give their loyalty to any one church. People of this class are not to be despised but to be pitied, for their toil is empty of meaning and sincerity. It is no wonder for they have never learned the secret of painstaking workmanship. They have never looked upon their labor as a reward in itself, merely as a means to other rewards. Theirs is probably a prayer of perpetual disillusion. They do not believe in work. They have no faith in what they are doing. They cannot put themselves wholeheartedly into it, and so they cry, "O that one would hear me! Behold my desire is that the Almighty would answer me."[41] And because the answer is work they do not recognize it. Their worship is not in sincerity, and in truth.

In the third place, there are still others whose worship is not all that could be desired. There are men and women who know exactly what they would like to do in this world, but for some reason or another are prevented from doing it. Either their ambitions outstrip their abilities, or their abilities go begging for lack of opportunity. There are women who would like to do the work of mothers and manage a household. There are wives who would like to have independent careers of their own. There are men who wish they had become lawyers or physicians or actors or editors or directors of a business of their own, but must continue to engage themselves in the work which has been thrust upon them, and which they perform with more or less inward rebellion. They feel that they are performing tasks that desecrate their souls, that deaden their finer sensibilities. To such as these, the daily round of cares and duties is something of a torment, and they find their greatest recreation not in work but in dreaming of the work that they had hoped and expected to perform. Theirs is indeed a prayer of

71

wistfulness. Like Naaman the servant in the Bible story, whose duty it was to be the King's escort at religious services in a faith that was not his own, they pray, "In this thing the Lord pardon thy servant that when my master goeth into the house of Rimmon to worship there, and he leaneth on my hand and I bow myself in the house of Rimmon, the Lord pardon thy servant in this thing." [42] There are people who feel the same way about their work, they feel like asking pardon of the God of the universe for not making full use of the talents and aptitudes which they believe they possess.

In the fourth place, there are those who while unsuccessful in discovering the work of their hearts, yet somehow manage to find peace and satisfaction in performing what is nearest at hand, and this class probably constitutes the bulk of humanity, and how fortunate it is. How fortunate it is that so many in this world have the wisdom to look upon their daily tasks as duties that must be performed, and who can find something more than complaint to make about their fate. It is true that their labor is more or less drudgery, but they have learned how much more blessed even drudgery is than a life of empty idleness. One of the great sermons preached by the late Dr. William C. Gannett was entitled, "Blessed be Drudgery." After the day's work is done genuine recreation can be found in rest. Theirs is the spiritual reward that comes only to those who know that they have actually earned their daily bread, so their prayer is a prayer of resignation, "I have learned, in whatsoever state I am, therewith to be content," [43] and they find a large measure of peace that comes from this resignation.

In the next place, there are the hypocrites, who worship to be seen of men, those who pretend to believe in work and recommend its practice to others but are not themselves engaged in any kind of labor, whether of hand or brain. Freed from the economic necessity to toil either by an overindulgent charity on the one hand or an economy of special privilege on the other, they try to make a business of doing nothing in particular, taking far more from the common storehouse of mankind than they ever expect to return. They are the idle rich and the idle poor. They constitute the great burden of shiftlessness, which the world's labor of brain and brawn lavishly support, and they can be found in every stratum of society. Theirs is today's greatest infidelity, for their prayers are sham and pretense. Of old time it has been said, "He who will not work shall not eat," but realistic religion proclaims, "He who will not work when he can, does not worship."

Finally, there are those who are actually engaged in the vocation of their heart's desire, who are doing what they want to be doing in this world, who are really in love with their work, who are not merely interested in getting the task done, but interested also in the very process of the task itself. These are the true sons and daughters of fortune, for their lives are full of worth and meaning, because their hands and brains are full of joyous employment. Their labor is not drudgery, their labor is not even a duty, it is a delight, and they find their receation not in dreams, nor even in rest, but their greatest recreation is in more work. Work to them becomes the most fascinating of all interests and concerns.

I shall never forget a certain policeman in Boston. This policeman was directing traffic at the foot of Beacon Hill in that city. I was fascinated by his performance, for he did not stand there like a mechanical robot, holding back half the traffic at one time and then signalling the other half to go forward. No, this man had brains, and his heart was in his work. He was more like an orchestra leader. With a wave of his hand and a nod of his head, he kept the traffic moving. He accelerated the speed of some, retarded the speed of others but kept every car in motion. There was no scowl on his face. He was an artist with a gleam in his eye for he enjoyed his work. His performance was something most fascinating to watch.

It was my privilege in college to be in the class of a professor of mathematics who would rather demonstrate a problem in trigonometry or calculus than go on a picnic. He just made mathematics dance. It was an inspiration to be in his class. I know of a mother who would rather keep house and work with her children than to do anything else

73

in the world; there is joy in her life, because there is joy in her labor. I used to know a lawyer, who would rather argue a case before a jury than to go fishing or hunting any time. He would postpone everything for an opportunity to go before a jury. Now every one no doubt could give several instances among friends of those who know what work they want to be doing in this world and are actually engaged in doing it. These are not only the true sons and daughters of fortune, they are the most effective worshippers of deity, for theirs is a prayer of genuine joy and thanksgiving.

Like the psalmist who said, "I was glad when they said unto me, let us go into the house of the Lord," [44] these people say, "I was glad when they said unto me, 'Let us go to work.'" Because their workmanship is painstaking, sincere, wholehearted, they are in possession of the deep satisfactions of life, they are better men for it. Every rise in the quality of labor that men perform is inevitably followed by a rise in the quality of the men that perform it. In the 13th century for example, when so many of the great cathedrals of Europe were being erected, most of the laborers on these structures, from the architects, and the masons, and the carpenters, down to the waterboys looked upon their respective vocations with such pride and reverence that it was one of the happiest of all times. There is only one other period in history that might have been happier, namely, the reign of King Asoka in India.

The time may yet come when this concept of toil as an act of worship is going to prevail once again, only on a grander and more widespread scale. Yes, a time is coming when man will strive above all things to count for something in this universe by seeking out a task which he may look upon as a religious ceremony. A time is coming when men will go forth to their daily occupations with the sublime consciousness that they are worshipping the great wonder of this universe in the most acceptable manner.

Achievement, creativity, bringing things to pass that never before existed—this seems to be the basic characteristic of the universe in which we live. This also constitutes the manifest destiny of man on earth.

Life is toil and all that lives
Sacrifice of labor gives.

Water, fire, and air and earth
Rest not, pause not from their birth,

Sacred toil doth nature share.
Love and labor-work is prayer.[45]

Chapter 9

MAN'S LIFE HAS AT LEAST ONE OBVIOUS PURPOSE

We are emphasizing the affirmative rather than the negative aspects of faith, and in this chapter we wish to affirm that life has at least one obvious purpose. What is that obvious purpose?

Let us take a look at life in the large to see whether it has some rational end in view. For here we are standing on the topmost peak of time with two of the most devastating wars in history behind us. From this vantage point we can view the teeming, striving, struggling world of humanity. In our mind's eye we can see men and women running to and fro in all parts of the globe, in this country and Europe, China, India, Australia, Africa, and the far-off isles of the sea—some to labor, some to rest from their labors, some to play and gamble and make merry, others to lay rough hands on their fellow man, some to worship in mosques and temples, and lift up joyous hearts in thanksgiving, others to curse the day they were born or to utter terrible threats against their neighbors.

We can see men and women lying on beds of pain, racked with sickness, crying out to heaven for help in their agony. We can see little children being born, some into homes of refinement and luxury, others into homes of filth and degradation. We can see weary millions, temporarily exiled trudging strange countrysides in search of a permanent abode. We can see lovers, enraptured by the mystery that draws them together, idealists faring forth to pursue an ever-receding goal, and we can see criminals plotting and scheming to hold a child for ransom or to break into some guarded structure and run off with the life savings of other men.

From this topmost peak of time, we can hear the strain of wedding marches, the tolling of bells announcing a funeral procession; we can hear the lullabies of mothers as they sing their infants to sleep in their arms, while they are interrupted by the crash of some terrible catastrophe and the groaning of wounded men and women.

In imagination we can see the responsible head of a major power wrestling with some fateful decision of foreign policy, pacing back and forth with his hands clasped behind his back and his head bent forward in serious meditation; and at the same moment and in the same realm a little child is crying over her broken doll, a grief stricken mother is standing bewildered besides an empty cradle, and an aged man with long white hair sits in the sun idly whittling a stick while wistfully dreaming of by-gone days.

What is the purpose behind it all? What is the end of life? Has it any discernible meaning? Has it any real goal? Now there are some people who have jumped to the conclusion that happiness must be that goal—that the meaning of life is to be found in the joy and blessedness it brings. But if happiness be that goal, if that be the purpose, then what a tragic mockery this world really is. For millions of people know little happiness from their first breath to their last; born in misery they grow up in the midst of sorrow and suffering. Their labor is drudgery! Their rewards are poor! They meet with sickness, accident, misfortune; they seldom have enough to eat; they go down to an untimely grave; and the tragedy of it all is as the poet says,

Not that they starve, but starve so dreamlessly;
Not that they sow but they seldom reap;
Not that they serve, but have no Gods to serve;
Not that they die, but that they die like sheep.[46]

If happiness be the purpose of life, then this world is a horrible blunder, a monstrous jest, a bitter hoax for millions of people. Even when people have all the creature comforts of life, happiness is by no means assured. The individuals who directly pursue it as an end in itself are more than likely

77

to miss it altogether, for there is none so far from happiness as he who thinks he is about to lay hands upon it. Anything so elusive, so unsubstantial, so incidental cannot possibly be an adequate explanation of the meaning of human existence. Happiness is to life what noiselessness is to an efficient motor, it is a sign that the machinery is working smoothly but it is not the reason why the machine was originally fashioned.

What then is the purpose of our life on this planet? Could it be the achievement of some highly perfected social order? Could the meaning of life be found in the progressive achievement of the kingdom of God on earth? If the happiness of individuals is not the obvious goal, perhaps it is the general welfare of humanity, a perfected state of human society. If so, then there must be something diabolical at loose in the universe wholly indifferent to such a goal.

H. G. Wells tells us that the Buddhist empire of King Asoka in the third century before Christ was the nearest approach to the kingdom of heaven on earth which history yet records.[47] Nevertheless the forces of life were allowed to crush that empire into the dust until there remains today nothing but the huge rock inscriptions in India, whereby the edicts of that empire were made known to the general public. Or let us take the Peruvian empire of the Ayar-Incas in South America before the coming of Columbus. It too had reached a high level of political, cultural, and economic welfare. Every man in that empire was guaranteed social security from the cradle to the grave, and safeguarded against the ordinary hazards of life. The general welfare was carefully and systematically planned for, and ten millions of people were more or less contented with their lot because there were long periods of peace so that they had no arms. It was an agricultural economy wherein these people domesticated and gave to the world more than a third of the present fruits and vegetables which we now enjoy in the western hemisphere—a wonderful civilization. Again the forces of life permitted this idealistic order to be crushed to the earth, and only the ruins of its mighty temples and gigantic irrigation projects remain to tell us of a glory that once was but is no more.[48]

In direct contrast to these highly organized political states, stands the early Roman republic and Merry England in the days of King Arthur, in both of which the social structure of government was very simple. There were few laws enacted, and therefore few laws to be disobeyed. The police power was seldom used and then most reluctantly. The individual enjoyed a large measure of personal freedom. Life was clean, wholesome, and uncomplicated. Some of us might well look on either social order, King Arthur's Merry England, or the early Roman republic as a reasonable replica of heaven on earth. But again the forces of life did not allow such ideal societies to remain in existence for very long. They too "had their day and ceased to be."

In this struggle for the perfection of human society, the world at large does not seem to be getting anywhere. Aristotle observed centuries ago that history seems to run in cycles. First we have a despotism, that is later on modified and becomes an oligarchy, and that may in turn be modified so as to bring about a republic or a democracy, and then it is the tendency of a democracy to degenerate into a mobocracy, a state of anarchy and chaos which brings forth the man on horseback who then starts the cycle all over again by setting up a new dictatorship. Democratic France has recently entrusted General De Gaulle with extraordinary powers. It remains to be seen whether he uses these powers wisely or abuses them as some of the would-be benevolent dictators of history have done. Yes, history seems to run in cycles. The author of Ecclesiastes says, "Behold there is nothing new under the sun. What has been is what will be. What has been done is what will be done."

Now do not misunderstand me at this point. It seems to me that the achievement of a better social order is indeed a most desirable goal—especially a better world in which war and the preparations of war have been completely outlawed. But I do not think there is anything permanent in such an achievement. For the gains of one millennium are quite likely to be lost in the next. For their conservation is apparently not automatically guaranteed by the nature of the universe. Sooner or later much of the achieving has to be done all over again. It seems to me then that anything so

79

temporary and fragile can scarcely explain the meaning of life, however worthwhile it may appeal to us as an immediate object of endeavor. It is often a temporary by-product of the struggle of life, but it cannot be its over-all purpose.

What then is the explanation of all man's striving and struggling? Is it as some biologists would maintain, the development of a higher species of physical life on this planet? There is much to be said for this point of view. Nature is obviously careless of individuals. It seems to be likewise careless of social systems. But does she not seem to be tremendously concerned about bringing forth ever new and better types. Dissatisfied with invertebrates, nature proceeded to develop vertebrates. Dissatisfied with fishes, she has created the amphibian, then the reptile, next the mammal, and then man; and out of man it may well be that eventually she will develop a superman that is yet to be. But when that superman shall come, what then? To what purpose has nature bent her efforts? To what goal has she run her race? For the days of superman on earth shall be numbered even as the days of his forebears were numbered.

In some distant time the warmth of the sun will grow cold. Summer will change to unending winter. The earth will become an iceberg, and there will be neither warmth nor bounteous harvest to support the life of superman. For we may well believe that even the supply of atomic energy will some day run out. Superman eventually will have to disappear as though he had never been, and unless somewhere and somehow nature is able to preserve some record of her achievements on this planet, we shall still have no adequate meaning whereby to explain the mystery of human existence. Perhaps there is no obvious purpose. Perhaps there is no discernible goal. Perhaps everything is as it is and will be what it will be without rhyme or reason. Perhaps after all, Macbeth's pessimism should prevail, "It is a tale told by an idiot, full of sound and fury, signifying nothing."

Perhaps after all, the meaning which we read into life has no other existence but in our own brains. Perhaps the whole thing is merely a subjective feeling, a foolish illusion of a feverish imagination. But if there is any obvious purpose, if there be any discernible meaning, I can see such a meaning and purpose in one thing only, namely, the achievement of character. This may not be the best possible of all worlds for such ends as individual happiness or a perfected society, or a perfected species, but it is almost ideal from the viewpoint of providing the stuff out of which character can be made. For here we have everything necessary to exercise the capacity of man's mind and spirit to the full. We have much sorrow to teach him the value of sympathy; much temptation to bring out the strength of his moral fiber; much frustration to train him in humility; much mystery to test his powers of faith; enough pain to teach him patience and forbearance. Every experience that man has to face on this planet from his first days of consciousness to his very last can be used by him as material for the building of character. For nothing is useless. Everything can be employed to advantage. The first frustration in the cradle, the toy that will not work, the disillusionment in discovering there is no Santa Claus, the reproof of parents, the scoffing of playmates, the death of relatives and friends, a disappointed love affair, a sudden provocation to anger, a lost opportunity, an unfortunate physical handicap, a prolonged illness, a distasteful task to perform, a burdensome responsibilty to shoulder, a terrible injustice to endure! All these experiences can be utilized with profit to the building up of skills and proficiencies of the human mind and spirit. But of course even such skills and proficiencies are but dust and ashes, are they not, if man's spirit is to perish with the frame of his body. Is not all still vanity of vanities if man himself is not to persist?

For me there must be some abiding quality to life, some permanence to give it adequate meaning. Even the achievement of character is something of a mockery if the spirit of man is to be snuffed out like the light of a candle. Reason requires the conservation of man's character to justify logically all the strain and stress of living. No other surmise can give meaning to this strange interlude between the cradle and the grave. But with this daring assumption, we can face all the vicissitudes of life with confidence and composure.

Has life any rational, obvious purpose? My answer is yes. If we have faith to believe that there is a kingdom within the soul of man that is an everlasting kingdom whose triumphs and achievements shall abide. There is evidence that such a kingdom exists. Psychologists and psychiatrists are telling us that we are what we are today because of our past experiences. While we may have consciously forgotten much of this experience, it is all registered in what has been called our subconscious memory. Nothing has been lost there, whether painful or pleasant, hopeful or discouraging, redemptive or degrading, sorrowful or joyous. The physical body which our life animates is not the body with which we were born. Many of us are old enough to have had several bodies. Yet with all our physical changes, some vital reality has remained a constant on which all these changes have been recorded, namely, the subconscious memory which is the indispensable link between our past, our present, and our future. I have faith that this memory which has survived all such changes in the past will survive the change called death —in short, that it is an indestructible page in the "Book of God's Remembrance"—and whatever has been written there is indelible and cannot be blotted out, but can only be amended by what we subsequently inscribe. For better or for worse, this is our character, our true self. This is the conclusion I have come to after thirty-five years of study of the findings of the American and British Societies for Psychical Research.

What then is the overall purpose of life? My answer is this—to achieve the best character possible—to give full rein to the potential Divinity within ourselves. This, in my judgment, is what it means "to glorify God and enjoy Him forever."

CHAPTER 10

WE HAVE A DUTY TO LOVE OURSELVES

Our hospitals for the mentally sick are filled to overflowing. Our present way of life, the total impact of our economic, political, and cultural institutions is producing such emotional tensions in our people that they are breaking down under the strain faster than our physicians and psychiatrists seem to be able to take care of them. Even people who give every outward sign of composure are often inwardly distraught, near the breaking point, because of a constant warfare being waged within their own minds and hearts.

How many times we have heard individuals confess that such is the pace of life today that they feel that they have been caught up in a "rat race"—they actually use that expression "rat race." There are those who may have great possessions, possessing everything they can possibly have any use for, except the one thing they crave most of all, namely, peace within themselves. Outwardly they are successful; inwardly they are living lives of more or less desperation. For example, there are some people who are running away from some childhood fear long since forgotten by the conscious mind, but a veritable demon with horns and hoofs in the subconscious, and they wear a haunted look. There are those who are being weighed down by some vague sense of guilt, perhaps acquired in the early years of life, which having never been faced openly or confessed or reexamined in the light of mature experience, lives on unresolved in the background of their imagination to bedevil their present joy, and becloud their present judgment. They have not learned how to forgive themselves, or how to go about it.

There are others who may be carrying on some foolish

rivalry with a brother, a sister, a father, a mother, or a friend, begun because of some painful experience in childhood, long since forgotten but still a dark and sinister driving impulse behind much of today's frantic struggling and striving. They have allowed childish fancies to direct mature ambitions, and they have not adjusted their ambitions to their abilities. Or they may be weeping inwardly over some inconsolable grief, which they were reluctant to give expression to at the time of its inception for one reason or another, but ever since have paid for their former negligence by a subconscious lamentation that constantly drains their vital spiritual energy. A past sorrow holds them in a merciless grip.

There are still others who may be looking desperately for a love and a spiritual security denied them in childhood, and because that early void was not normally filled at the time, it has grown ever since with the years until no amount of subsequent affection can begin to fill it, or they have acquired an abnormal appetite for love and attention which cannot be normally satisfied. There are people who actually hate themselves, and who are really their own worst enemy for they do cruel things to themselves. They punish themselves in various ways without fully realizing it.

The deep findings of modern psychology reveal that some suicides may be an atonement that a vindictive conscience imposes upon the self-killer. He wishes to expiate his crime, usually some infantile indiscretion, and does so upon the altar of his own body.

Yes, there are people in the world who are constantly at warfare within themselves; some literally hating themselves to such an extent that it is unsafe to allow them to become parents or teachers, or companions of our children, for they have neglected one of the important duties of life, namely, the obligations to be just and kind to themselves.

In the second of the great commandments in which Jesus summed up the law and the prophets, there is implied a third important commandment which organized religion has only vaguely understood, even to date. The first, of course, is the love of God, the love of life and the wonder of it all. The second the love of one's neighbor, who is part of this wonder, but the third, indeed logically it should come second, is the love of one's self as made in the image of God, made certainly in the image of something wondrous. Now some may object that this is no commandment at all, that when Jesus said, "Love thy neighbor as thyself," he had no intention of enjoining the love of self because forsooth he had the right to take for granted that all men just naturally look out for themselves, and why enjoin them to do something which they cannot keep from doing. But the truth of the matter is that there are some people who do not naturally love themselves. Now just as there is a selfish love of others, so there is an unselfish love of one's self. Parents sometimes have a selfish love for their children. Their feeling for them is more for the sheer delight that such an affection gives them than because of any real devotion to the child's true welfare. This is frequently seen in those instances where parents take too dominating a part in shaping the careers of their own sons and daughters, especially when they insist upon them settling down near home, even when it is at the expense of jeopardizing their present or their future opportunities. Sometimes we love others not for their sake but for our own.

Much of our boasted philanthropy in the world today in helping needy nations is also a selfish love of others. We are helping many of the needy nations today, not for their sakes, but because we wish to keep them on our own side in the present struggle. Granted that it is intelligent selfishness, nevertheless behind it lies the ulterior motive. Long before the days of Jesus it had been well understood that there were not only those who pray to be seen of men, but also those who give alms to be seen of men, who serve only to be well thought of. Yes, there is undoubtedly such a thing as the selfish love of others, but by the same token, there is likewise the unselfish love of ourselves. He who loves himself, as Jesus and the great Hebrew prophets before him implied, is under the obligation to protect and develop the capacities of his personal life as an endowment of infinite worth. Or as Shakespeare put it, "This above all to thine ownself be true, and it must follow as the night the day thou canst not then be false to any man." A decent concern for ourselves is the indispensable prerequisite of being able to serve our fellow men. As someone has so well observed—"What boots it if we give ourselves to others if we have no self worth giving? Of what avail is it to let our light shine before men if our light within is darkness? To what purpose do we love our neighbor as ourselves, if we do not love ourselves intelligently or permit our love to turn to hatred, revenge, and destructive impulses against our deepest natures?" The quality of the service which people are capable of rendering to others depends very much on the quality of the servant.

Therefore, we all have a definite obligation to cultivate our inner life, not only for our own sake but for the sake of others. People who suffer from inferiority complexes or from martyr complexes are obsessed by some deep deep sense of fear or guilt; they are forever fighting unrealistic battles in the shadow land of their own subconscious. In short, people who have never achieved a wholesome spirit within themselves seldom realize what an extra burden they are to their friends and loved ones and all who have to live with them or work with them. They seldom realize how they complicate the problems of others. Some of them are aware and would like to do something about it, but they do not know how. Here is where modern psychology comes in and can be of considerable help. It is a most difficult task to attain that integrity of personality, that wholeness of personality wherein our major conflicting ambitions and desires have been resolved. For will power and sheer resolution alone will not avail as many have found out. Something else is necessary, namely, a deep searching of our own hearts.

We could all afford to take more time for a deep searching of our own hearts and if necessary to call on the assistance of experts to help us to uncover what it is that is disturbing our self-assurance and self-respect. The reformation of this world must begin with the reformation of ourselves. We should all aim to achieve a mature character. Ethical religion has always emphasized the achieving of character. People have got to *be* something before they can help others very much.

There are parents today who have been so busy doing

things for their children, so anxious to give them everything they need that they have overlooked the most needful gift of all, namely, the example of parents who have achieved a well-rounded personality for themselves.

There are teachers who have literally exhausted themselves in looking out for the interests of their pupils that they have lost much of the original charm they once possessed and have allowed themselves to acquire mannerisms that betray inward tension and impatience.

There are clergymen who have become so bogged down with the duties of parish administration and parish calling that they have neglected the enrichment of their own minds, and when they rise to speak have little more than platitudes with which to inspire their congregations.

There are editors, lawyers, doctors, business men and labor leaders so anxious to serve their fellowmen and have become so exhausted in so doing that they unwittingly spread the exhaustion they feel wherever they go, and especially in the circles of their own homes.

As the gift without the giver is bare, so is much of the service that some people render. In our eagerness to *do* for others we should not overlook the obligation to *be* something to them. What a relief it is to come into the presence of those who have made this important discovery and responded accordingly. Just to be with them is to feel a greater sense of personal security. They may possess considerable knowledge, but they do not make us ashamed of the less knowledge we may possess. They understand our faults and limitations and do not run us down and make us admit that we have erred when we have. Through the years they have mastered their own tempers and therefore are able to calm the tempestuous emotions in ourselves. Pay them a compliment and they do not react with flippancy or condescension but with gracious appreciation, making us feel glad that we took the pains to compliment them. We go to them for advice, but instead of giving it they encourage us to talk over our problems so thoroughly that the solution becomes obvious to us and it is our own advice that we finally take.

There was an American chaplain, stationed in Dijon,

France during the first World War, whom it was a privilege to know. He made a deep impression upon many. I have forgotten his name but I can never forget his face or his voice. He was a man of natural dignity—simple and unassuming—but how rich he was in treasures of the mind and heart! While an atmosphere of hurry and excitement prevailed all about him, he himself was ever calm and unhurried—never so busy that he could not drop at once whatever he was doing to extend a hearty and gracious welcome to his visitor. He said very little, but he listened most intently, venturing a short and relevant comment only now and then. But one went from his presence with a sense of having been blessed and exalted.

Yes, there are those who are able to relieve our anxieties and tensions by their own confident manner and radiant spirit. To achieve such composure is a purpose surely worthy of all we can give it.

Perhaps no one can achieve complete love and respect for himself without first being possessed by an overall confidence in the underlying purpose behind our life on this planet, what all religions have defined as a living faith, the kind of faith that inspired Isaiah to declare, "Thou wilt keep him in perfect peace whose mind is stayed on thee"; which impelled the poet, Edwin Markham, to write his poem entitled "The Place of Peace."

> At the heart of the cyclone tearing the sky,
> And flinging the clouds and towers by,
> Is a central calm.
>
> So here in the roar of mortal things,
> I have found a place where my spirit sings,
> In the hollow of God's Palm.[49]

Now some may be as reluctant as I am to use the expression, "In the hollow of God's Palm" because of its physical connotations, but whether we call ourselves humanists or theists, whether we are able to personify the wondrous life behind our own, or are able only to apostrophize this life in terms of law and principle, we shall probably not be able to

love and respect ourselves adequately until we have first fulfilled our duty to achieve an outlook on the mystery of life
that is the spiritual equivalent of that radiancy exemplified by
Isaiah, Jesus, and Edwin Markham, but also exemplified by
Buddha, Confucius, and Laotze who were fundamentally humanists in their overall point of view. It is the moral equivalent
of this faith that has been vouchsafed to theist and humanist
alike which seems to be necessary before we can fully love
and reverence the life within ourselves.

CHAPTER 11

MODERN MAN NEEDS A SENSE OF SIN

The word "sin" is fast dropping out of the vocabulary of modern man and even from the vocabulary of the modern pulpit. Of course we are all opposed to sin or "agin it" to use the expression of Calvin Coolidge, but to mention the word "sin" today is to raise more smiles than to convey any definite meaning in spite of the fact that the concept of sin is basic in both the old and new testaments.

In this respect, a clear contrast exists between the religion of our forefathers and much of the religion of today. To our forefathers, sin was a terrifying reality and salvation from sin was a major concern. They were taught to believe that all men are depraved—that when they were born they inherited an awful guilt transmitted to them by the disobedience of Adam and Eve in eating the forbidden fruit of the tree of the knowledge of good and evil which grew in the Garden of Eden. They were taught to believe that no matter how much they may have striven to live a righteous life, there was absolutely nothing they could do to remove the mortal curse laid upon all humanity except to rely upon the grace of Almighty God and publicly confess and accept Jesus Christ as his only begotten son, who died on Calvary as an atonement for the original sin of Adam and Eve as well as for their own sin.

Even little children before they were old enough to know anything at all, let alone the meaning of sin, were regarded in certain religious circles as much in need of salvation as the most hardened criminal and accordingly were believed to be destined for an eternal hell of torment if they happened to die without being baptized.

Against this monstrous doctrine of original sin and mechanical salvation there was bound to arise eventually a mighty protest. Over a hundred and fifty years ago men like William Ellery Channing, Hosea Ballou and Joseph Priestley began to proclaim the essential goodness of human nature. They vigorously denied the doctrine of man's depravity as proclaimed by John Calvin and Jonathan Edwards and affirmed instead the more hopeful doctrine of man's potential divinity.

They contended that man is not "a worm in the dust," but rather an angel not yet fully developed—not a child of the devil but a son of God—his soul stamped with the image of the Eternal One and therefore invested with an immortal destiny. Man, they granted, was far from being perfect. He had his faults and shortcomings, his lapses and his excesses, but much of the evil in him was due to a hostile environment and a badly organized system of society. Human nature, they argued, does not need so much to be changed as to be given a chance.

Let the institutions of society be altered, let the environment of man be improved and man's potential goodness will eventually blossom forth as a rose in a cultivated garden. The process of enfoldment will necessarily take an indefinite number of generations—much patience must be shown toward those who fail to respond, but no one should be despaired of for man is destined for progress forever onward and upward.

Under this exalted view of human nature, many Americans were brought up and even those who were brought up in the orthodox faith were given a picture of human nature that reflected the mollifying influence of this generous and optimistic faith. For during the past sixty to seventy years this idea spread most rapidly. It permeated much of the literature and general culture of our times. An increasing number of those within the church as well as the great majority of those outside the church can no longer subscribe to the doctrine of man's depravity. The vivid sense of sin which once possessed our forefathers has now been all but replaced by what amounts to an optimistic view of human nature.

It is precisely at this point that many modern theologians have entered a protest. They hold that the wholesome reaction against the doctrine of man's depravity, which began over a hundred and fifty years ago has now swung too far and has reached an extreme where the prevailing view of human nature is just as fantastic, distorted and unrealistic as that of John Calvin and Jonathan Edwards. While it is true that those theologians grossly exaggerated man's innate depravity, it is equally true that we have grossly exaggerated man's innate divinity—while they were morbidly over-conscious of sin we have become complacently under-conscious—while their view of human nature was too harsh and pessimistic, ours has become too indulgent and optimistic—while they believed that human nature was too far sunk in sin to be saved except by special intervention from heaven, we have come to believe that human nature is so close to divinity as to be almost in no need of salvation. What wonder, it is argued, that we are hearing today such expressions of moral irresponsibility as the following:

One person is just as good as another.
Why shouldn't I do what I please?
How do we determine what is right and wrong?
Does anyone really know?
Is it not all a matter of relativity anyhow?
The thing to do is to express oneself.
Why speak of salvation?
What is there to be saved from?
Morality is a matter of custom and convenience.

Why become exercised about something concerning which there is no final word of authority? In short, how one lives his life is entirely one's own private affair so long as one minds his own business.

In this blasé attitude, which is not uncommon, we see how current opinion in its view of the reality of sin has almost completely swung to the opposite extreme of what once prevailed.

And yet, it seems to me, there is such a thing as the reality of sin. One has but to look upon the colossal ruination and widespread misery which two world wars brought and the awful wastefulness of natural and human resources involved in the present armament race which the Cold War has brought (and all within the power of man to prevent) to realize that there is such a thing as the reality of sin.

However much we may dislike the word because of its former theological connotations, we are not realists if we overlook the fact that there is after all something in man from which he needs to be redeemed. Call it moral inertia, man's natural selfishness and greed or some other euphonious name, but let us not blind ourselves to the tragic fact that there is in man a certain potential for perversity that frequently turns his finest endeavors into failures, his fairest dreams into ashes, and his most glorious achievements into sorrowful disillusionments. How naïve and superficial we have been in our thinking! For it was once thought that if we only had the secret ballot the Kingdom of Heaven on earth would be just around the corner—then in turn it was thought that if we only had the direct primary, woman's suffrage, the League of Nations, the United Nations, at least the beginnings of the Kingdom would be in sight. Surely we must have overlooked something important in our calculations, namely, the duality of human nature.

Yes, man has inherited from the past not only potentialities for good but also potentialities for evil. The old doctrine of original sin and all its implications of mechanical salvation must be given up, but a new doctrine of original sin, sin as evil tendencies inherited from jungle ancestors, must be clearly recognized. Modern psychology holds that there are deep-seated destructive impulses in most of us, impulses that once had considerable survival value in man's more primitive stages of development, but which in today's more complex and interdependent world threatens the survival of the human race.

If the behavior of man in the recent past is any indication of his conduct in the future, no invention, no political device, no social scheme is likely to perform the task of ridding the world of evil by and of itself. No! not until man first makes a greater success of ridding evil from his own heart and this he can not do without frankly facing the fact that there is evil there from which he needs to be redeemed, and that the responsibility for beginning this redemption lies primarily within himself.

Socrates was of the opinion that man needs only to know the right to embrace it—that unrighteousness is largely a matter of ignorance and lack of education. Christopher Marlowe in his prologue to *The Jew of Malta* declares, "There is no sin but ignorance." But this can not be the whole truth for there are men and women in this world who know what is right but deliberately turn away from doing it. We know this to be true because we know it to be a fact in our own lives. We know only too well how often we pray for more light when we do not follow the light which we already have. We can not believe, therefore, that all the revolting crimes and atrocities which have been perpetrated by man against his fellowman during our lifetime can be explained on the extenuating basis of ignorance. No, there have been men and women who have known that what they were doing was evil but have chosen to do it just the same.

Jesus looked with compassion on the soldiers who nailed him to his cross, saying, "Father, forgive them for they know not what they do." [50] They probably thought they were merely doing their duty for they had been taught to obey orders. But there is no record of Jesus asking forgiveness for Pilate and Caiaphas and the other high officials who ordered his crucifixion. They undoubtedly knew what they were doing and that it was evil. Pilate is reported to have said, "I find in him no fault at all." [51] He and those who connived in bringing the trumped-up charges against Jesus were the ones morally responsible. Even so we may well believe that Jesus, being the character he was, would have asked forgiveness for Pilate and Caiaphas had they shown any signs of true repentance.

No, this world can not get along without the concept of man's moral responsibility for the evil he deliberately commits. The concept of sin, however, involves something more than crimes, immorality, or vice. One may be free from crime, immorality and vice and still be guilty of sin.

Roughly speaking, crime is defiance of the laws of the state; immorality is defiance of the ethical sanctions of society; vice is defiance of the laws of physical well being; sin is defiance of the will of God.

Now, what do we mean by defiance of the will of God? What we mean is vitally and logically related to our concept of Deity. Since the liberal has given up the idea of a supernatural God, he has likewise given up the idea that sin is defiance of any of the codes of behavior alleged to have been supernaturally revealed.

Since he communes with an indwelling Deity, he looks upon sin as the failure to live our lives according to the inner light which we behold within ourselves. That light may vary in brightness with each individual, but the extent to which we go contrary to that light is the measure of our sin, and it is sin in the religious sense of disobedience to the will of God.

Every inward revelation of truth, every conviction of what is right, every vision of the more beautiful we may have imposes an obligation upon us to obey. To disobey is indeed to defy the creative power of this universe and thus to delay and impede the divine unfoldment of life. "Whoever knows what is right to do and fails to do it, for him it is sin." [52]

In this sense, it is no exaggeration to say that we have all sinned and come short of the glory of God. "We have left undone those things which we ought to have done and we have done those things which we ought to have left undone." It is interesting to note that it is not those the world calls its greatest sinners who have been the most conscious of guilt, but those it has been inspired to call its greatest saints. Paul, Augustine, Francis of Assisi, Henry Drummond, Leo Tolstoi, Kagawa, Gandhi—all confessed to a keen sense of sin. Jesus can not be wholly an exception for when a certain ruler in Israel once addressed him as Good Master, Jesus is reported to have replied, "Why callest thou me good? None is good save one, that is, God." (Luke 18:19)

One of the memories which brought remorse to the

Apostle Paul was that of the occasion when Stephen was stoned to death and he had tacitly connived in the brutal affair or, as he expressed it, "And when the blood of thy martyr Stephen was shed, I also was standing by and consenting unto his death and kept the raiments of them that slew him." [53]

To what extent have we all stood by consenting to the evils of our own day? When we consider the numberless cruelties and atrocities of our age, its horrifying sacrifice of youth on the altar of war, its alarming blood-thirstiness and relapse into barbaric practices, its callous repression of fundamental human rights, its inhumanity to man that has orphaned the innocent and made countless thousands mourn, and how every one of us have been more or less involved in this corporate evil of our time, either directly by participating in war, violence and repression or indirectly by wanting the things that make for war, violence and repression, then we must confess before the God of the Highest within ourselves our share in the guilt of the world. For we have all sinned in that we have stood by consenting to a greater or lesser degree or have kept the garments of them that slew.

"The only thing necessary for the triumph of evil is for good men to do nothing," wrote Edmund Burke in a private letter to his friend Thomas Merch.[54] A wise man of Athens was once asked when injustice would be abolished. He replied, "When those who are not wronged wax as indignant as those who are." And George Bernard Shaw has declared, "The worst sin towards our fellow creatures is not to hate them but to be indifferent to them; that is the essence of inhumanity." [55]

Even if we have not participated directly in sins of commission, our sins of omission, if we had an imagination commensurate with our share in the evil of our times, should fill us with the kind of humility that characterized the Psalmist when he cried:

> Have mercy upon me, O God, according to thy loving kindness; according unto the multitude of thy tender mercies blot out my transgression.

Wash me thoroughly from mine iniquity, and cleanse me from my sin.

For I acknowledge my transgressions; and my sin is ever before me.

Against thee, thee only have I sinned, and done this evil in thy sight. . . .

Behold, thou desirest truth in the inward parts; and in the hidden part thou shalt make me to know wisdom. . . .

Create in me a clean heart, O God; and renew a right spirit within me.[56]

Only the individual directly involved is in a position to appraise how far short he has come of the glory within himself. The sense of sin needed is that by which to judge ourselves, not to judge others. If genuine, it should make us not more self-righteous but more humble—not less but more sympathetic toward all mankind.

CHAPTER 12

HOW WE JUDGE OTHERS REVEALS WHAT
WE ARE

"Judge not, that ye be not judged, for with what judgment
ye judge ye shall be judged, and with what measure ye mete
it shall be measured to you again." [56a]

When Jesus of Nazareth uttered these words He anticipated the findings of modern psychology. Nineteen hundred
years ago, without the benefit of the discoveries of Freud,
Jung and Adler, a carpenter from a remote village in Northern
Galilee saw clearly into the complicated mechanism of the
human mind, and noted how subtle and devious are its ways.
And nowhere does Jesus display this understanding with
greater profundity than in the spiritual insight which constitutes the theme of this chapter,—"Judge not, that ye be
not judged."

How prone is man to find fault with his brother man!
How much easier it is for him to see the "mote" in another's
eye and overlook "the beam" in his own! Scarcely a day ever
goes by that most of us do not pronounce judgment on
someone else, either audibly to that individual or about that
individual to another or inaudibly to ourselves. And, I mean
by judgment, what the context clearly implies: harsh, unfair,
impatient and unsympathetic criticisms. How often, finding
fault with others is merely a face-saving device to keep from
discovering our own faults. Now the average individual
desires nothing quite so much in this world as to seem
important in his own eyes. And what could be more natural
for him than to try to inflate this feeling of importance
by running someone else down. This is an ever present
temptation, a temptation difficult to resist. Yet lasting harm

can often result from our hasty and ill-considered judgments one of another.

I had a classmate during my second year in Divinity School who was once unjustly accused by an overly suspicious fellow student of having cheated in his examination. The honor system prevailed there at that time. The professor giving the examination is present at the beginning in order to give out the questions, but soon after he leaves the room and does not return until the end of the period. Every man writes somewhere on his paper: "I have neither given nor received aid" and signs his name. Now my classmate in the course of his examination was seen to take out several sheets of paper from his pocket to read, then to go back and finish the examination. And this over-suspicious student noticed it and reported the incident to the Dean, who summoned my friend to explain his action. I was finally called in to give my testimony, for the Dean understood that I had known my friend for a long time, even in my college days. He was a brilliant student. He had not only gone through college in three years but had achieved a master's degree in that same period, graduating not only with Phi Beta Kappa honors but also Summa Cum Laude. He possessed a photographic memory, and was so naturally brilliant that he never had any reason to cheat in an examination. I had never in all my years of knowing him observed a single instance where he had displayed any trait of dishonesty. He was the soul of honor. This is what happened. Just before going into the three-hour examination he had received a letter in the morning mail from the woman he was later to marry. He had had time only to glance through the letter when he had to go into his examination. When he had answered most of the questions and saw that all the rest could be answered rather easily, and that there was plenty of time to do so, he took time out to finish reading his half-read letter, and then he went back to the examination. Of course, this was a thoughtless thing for him to do under the circumstances, but he was so innocent of wrong-doing that he had not given a thought to it. I noticed the same thing—I did not give any thought to it, but apparently this other overly-suspicious student thought it

99

was his duty to report it. I do not mean to judge him nor the motives behind it. My testimony completely exonerated my friend in the judgment of the Dean. But the fact that his honesty had been questioned at all was a cruel wound from which he never fully recovered. It troubled him even up to the time of his death a few years ago.

Yes, there is always danger of doing a great injury in pronouncing judgment upon another because we seldom have all the facts and never know whether we have or not. But this is not the major reason for refraining from judgment of one another, according to the insight of Jesus. "With what judgment ye judge ye shall be judged." No, it is not merely the injury that we bring to others but the injury that we do to ourselves. This is what was behind the injunction of Jesus. The habit of finding fault with our brother is an urgent invitation for him to find fault with us. Disparagement of others begets disparagement of ourselves. If we would avoid unkindly, unjust, impatient, harsh criticism of ourselves, then we must see to it that we are not guilty of the same thing. No one likes to have his motives misconstrued. No one likes to have his foibles magnified into sins and flaunted before his own face and especially before the faces of others. No one likes to have his virtues taken for vices. As we would that others should do to us so we should do to them. And how often the very individual who goes about making harsh, unfair remarks about his intimate friends is most startled and pained when the tables are turned against himself.

Now, what Jesus is warning against is not *all* judgments, for society could not function without some evaluations of persons and motivations. Our community and our nation could not get very far without the constant exercise of the critical faculty. Deliberate preference must be shown for certain leaders and candidates over against others. And considerable care must be taken by our courts as to what citizens should be allowed freedom if the safety of the greatest number is to be preserved. No, what Jesus is warning against is not all judgments but unfair, harsh, hasty, ill-considered judgments—the habit of censoriousness which is a self-punishing habit because it is more than likely to provoke retaliations in kind.

Even yet, we have not arrived at the major import of what Jesus must have had in mind. His discernment into the workings of human nature was much more profound than appears on the surface. The clue to his discernment is to be found in the word "hypocrite." Judge not, because it brings harm to others? Yes. Judge not, because it often provokes retaliations in kind upon ourselves? Yes. But judge not because it is also a self-incriminating procedure. Judge not, that ye be not judged. The very fault that we condemn in others is more likely to be the fault in ourselves that is giving us the most trouble. In fact, the more a certain fault in our brother or our neighbor or our friend seems to trouble us, especially if it arouses our emotions, the more likely it is that we possess that fault to a marked degree. "Why beholdest thou the mote that is in thy brother's eye but considerest not the beam that is in thine own eye? Thou hypocrite, cast out first the beam that is in thine own eye, and then thou shalt see clearly to cast out the mote out of thy brother's eye." James Moffat in his translation says: "Thou hypocrite, cast out first the plank that is in thine own eye, and then thou shall see clearly to cast out the splinter that is in thy brother's eye,"—the plank and the splinter being of the same material.

The evil trait in another which arouses our ire, and in proportion as it arouses our ire, is indicative of the potential presence of the same or similar trait within our own character. Psychologists claim that the evil mind as a rule attributes to others the same vice that is in its own subconsciousness. For instance, the excessive prude is likely to be at heart a sensualist. The man who cannot credit others with telling the truth is likely to be himself a liar. The paranoid who believes that he is subject to the hatred of those about him feels that way simply because of the hatred in his own soul. Jesus said as much.

Jesus once came upon a crowd of men about to stone a woman caught in the very act of adultery. The self-righteousness with which these men were going about their task of stoning this woman was a clear sign to Jesus that these men were merely trying to escape a feeling of guilt for either adulterous acts or adulterous thoughts, so He boldly said to them, "He that is without sin among you, let him first cast a stone at her." [57] And one by one they slunk away until no one was left but Jesus and the woman, and he, who was not conscious of guilt, refused to pronounce judgment upon her. Let us beware how we pronounce judgments against one another. For in no way do we so clearly reveal our own shortcomings, if not to ourselves, surely to those who have any understanding about the strange ways of the human heart.

Another story about Jesus emphasizes this same point. It is the story of the two brothers who were present at one of his outdoor meetings. At the close, the younger brother said to Jesus: "Speak to my brother that he divide the inheritance with me." And Jesus replied: "Who made me a judge and divider over you? Beware of all covetousness. A man's life consisteth not in the abundance of things he possesseth." You see, the very greed with which the younger brother complained about in his older brother, was also in his own heart, as clearly evidenced by his willingness to air a private grievance in public.

It is not people without fault who find the most fault, but rather those who possess the most faults themselves. We have all heard the proverb, "It takes a thief to catch a thief." By the same token, it takes a liar to suspect a liar. He who likes to run other people into a corner and make them confess they have told an untruth, had better begin to search for the dishonesty in his own heart. He who finds it easy to make reckless charges of bigotry against his fellow man bears watching. He is often among the worst bigots. He who thinks that everyone has his price, has probably at some time sold out himself. If we find ourselves wishing that we could boil a certain individual in oil, before boiling him, we had better find out first what it is in his character that makes us want to boil him, and then look for that very trait in our own character. For the sin which we find most difficult to forgive in another is never wholly extraneous to ourselves.

102

It is more than likely to be the sin in our own lives for which we have never forgiven ourselves—if not the same sin, a very close relative.

I am sure that many are familiar with the couplet by Samuel Butler who describes "those who compound for sins they are inclined to, by damning those they have no mind to." Now, that is probably true as far as the sins of which men are conscious. But I think it is equally true that if there is emotional venom in our damning sins we have no mind to, or we think we have no mind to, we better have a second thought, for those are likely to be the very sins we *are* inclined to. I take it that this is the meaning of Jesus' reference to the beam in our own eye. Someone has observed that whenever we are tempted to point the finger of condemnation at another, we do not use the open hand, with all our fingers outstretched. No, we use the idex finger in pointing at the individual while three other fingers point at ourselves. That is generally the gesture. Now, I am not arguing that there is any necessary causal relation between the attitude of condemnation of ourselves and the three fingers turned toward ourselves in this instinctive action. I am merely suggesting, rather, that whenever we point the finger of condemnation at another, and we also at the same time feel a marked feeling of self-righteousness, then we had better look for some significance in the three fingers pointing toward ourselves. We had better plead the fifth amendment, if you please, and protect ourselves from giving self-incriminating evidence.

We are periodically confronted by political campaigns in which the evaluation of candidates and parties is a necessary function of our democracy. Whichever way we intend to cast our ballot let us be as fair to the other side as possible, and especially let us be fair to our friends and acquaintances who may be supporting a side different from our own. There will be the temptation to impugn the motives, to disparage the intelligence of those who may disagree with our conclusions. There will be the temptation to relay trivial tales about the various candidates, to argue by innuendo and to make sweeping generalizations on flimsy hearsay evidence. There will certainly be the temptation to use angry and exaggerated language, to communicate to our friends or our opponents not how we think but how we feel. Someone has said that the difference between a conviction and a prejudice is that you can explain a conviction without "getting hot under the collar." Let us be on guard against all petty and ill-considered judgments of candidates and of our friends of the opposition party, lest we betray how unworthy we are to exercise the rights of suffrage in our great democracy.

Yes, in all our relations one with another, especially in our relations at home, at work, church, school and club, there is room for more generous appraisal of one another, is there not? The French have a proverb that, "To know all is to forgive all," but the old Russian peasant had a proverb that goes even further: "To know all is to know that there is nothing to forgive." Bertrand Russell comes to essentially the same conclusion when he says:

> The life of man is a long march through the night toward a goal which few can hope to reach. One by one as they march, our comrades vanish from our sight. Very brief is the time in which we can help them, in which their happiness or misery is decided. Therefore, let us not weigh in grudging scales their merits, but let us think only of their needs, let us remember that they are fellow sufferers in the same darkness, actors in the same tragedy, with ourselves. And so, when their day is over, when their good and their evil have become eternal by the immortality of the past, be it ours to feel that where they suffered, where they failed, no deed of ours was the cause, but whenever the spark of divine fire kindled in their hearts, we were ready with encouragement, with sympathy, with brave words in which high courage glows.[58]

CHAPTER 13

WE ARE PRONE TO DESTROY WHAT WE LOVE

We are all tempted to destroy what we most love. This thought is suggested by Oscar Wilde's well known poem entitled, "The Ballad of Reading Gaol." In this poem, the author describes the restlessness of a certain prisoner in Reading Gaol frantically pacing back and forth in his prison cell, awaiting execution for the crime of murdering his wife. He is frantic, not so much from fear of what is about to be done to him as from remorse for what he himself had already done to another. For, as the poem explains,

The man had killed the thing he loved, and then goes on to observe:

> Yet each man kills the thing he loves,
> By each let this be heard.
> Some do it with a bitter look,
> Some with a flattering word,
> The coward does it with a kiss,
> The brave man with a sword.[59]

Yes, deep down in the human heart there are strange wild destructive impulses to take the very life of that which we love the most. So deep-lying are these impulses that they seldom come to consciousness, with the result that many of us go on destroying the thing we love without ever realizing what we are doing.

It was the terrible fate of that prisoner in Reading Gaol to know what he had done. In a fit of blind rage, he had killed the one person in all the world who had made life meaningful for him. And his heart was torn with the agony of grief and remorse.

King David of ancient Israel knew a similar agony. His favorite son was Absalom, the pride and joy of his life. And yet King David was responsible for that son's tragic end. It was not his own spear, to be sure, that pierced his son's heart—Joab, the chief of his armies, had done that. Yet when news of Absalom's fate was brought to the King, David fully realized that he himself was responsible, for he and he alone had set in motion the train of events which had led directly to the death of his son. Instead of blaming others, David went up to his chambers and wept bitter tears, crying in his agony—

O my son Absalom, my son, my son Absalom! Would that I had died for thee, O Absalom, my son, my son! [60]

The remorse of King David, as well as that of the prisoner in Reading Gaol, was immediate and overpowering, because in each case there was tangible evidence of the crime committed and the loss sustained.

But there are many ways of destroying the thing we love besides effecting its physical destruction. There is such a crime, for example, as spiritual homicide. It is precisely here in the realm of spiritual values where every one of us needs to be on guard against his own destructive tendencies.

Here is a man who marries the woman of his choice. What is the one quality in her life which has attracted him above all others? It is her maternal nature. The instinct of tenderness in her is very strong. If she had not possessed this virtue, he would not have married her in the first place. Children are born, and these children in time require more and more of the mother's attention. The father begins to begrudge the amount of this attention. In various ways he sets out to change the character of his wife by sarcastic remarks, or angry altercations, or silent neglect, until he has so transformed her natural tenderness into something hard and unyielding that he succeeds in destroying the very quality in her which he cherishes the most.

Here is a woman who marries the man of her choice. What is the one virtue in his life which has attracted her above all others? It is his chivalrous manner—the gallant way in which he conducts himself in the presence of other people—his buoyant spirit and complete lack of self-consciousness. They marry, and then what does she do but proceed to criticize the very quality in him which had originally won her heart. Out of fear or other motive, she begrudges him the most harmless attentions to other men and women. She finds fault not with his vices so much as with his chief virtue. By her constant jealousy she makes him so self-conscious and so much on his guard that he becomes an entirely different personality. And then when it is too late, she becomes vaguely aware that something beautiful has gone out of her life—but not sufficiently aware to realize that she alone has been largely responsible for her fate. As one of our poets has described this kind of tragedy—

It isn't Love's going that haunts my days,
It's just because it went in such little ways.

Or again, here is a child who is the very life and joy of a parent. What is the one quality in this child which is most obvious and lovable? It is his natural honesty—his frank and open countenance—his instinctive reluctance either to tell or act a lie.

But the parent does not realize that as his child advances in years, there is need for more and more privacy if honesty would remain honest. The solicitous supervision that was once beneficial in infancy would become a tyrannical and destructive force as the child grows older. There are times when certain direct personal questions should not be asked of any child.

By an overweening curiosity to know everything that our children are doing or have done, there is grave peril of turning them into accomplished prevaricators. We tempt them to deceive us by begrudging them the privacy essential to their own spiritual growth and thus succeed in destroying in them that which we once prized so highly.

And this is just as true of our friendships. By keeping too close a watch over our friends, by trailing their movements too minutely and asking questions which we have no right to ask, we often undermine the very trust that makes the relationship possible and then lament the loss which is ours without even surmising our own share in bringing it about.

Yes, there are many ways in which we are prone to destroy the thing we love,—the possessive attitude, the bitter look, the sarcastic repartee, the yawn of indifference, the rebuke of ridicule, the nagging spirit. How we sometimes wish we could go back to a certain period in our lives and start all over again with what we now know! How we wish we could reclaim values which once were ours but are now lost, perhaps forever!

In no sphere of life is there greater danger of destroying what we treasure than in the sphere of religion. Men have had a profound spiritual experience—some revelation of ethical insight—some mystical companionship with things eternal and unseen, and then have sought to preserve it for the inspiration of future generations in the form of rituals, creeds, and ceremonies.

That which the prophet and seer have discovered, the priest and ecclesiastic would organize and systematize. But in so doing they run a serious risk of losing the thing they would preserve. They do not seem to realize how the letter killeth while it is the spirit that giveth life.

John Steinbeck in his revealing novel *Of Mice and Men*, describes a half-wit who loves to stroke the soft fur of little animals. But he holds them so tightly that he crushes out their life without realizing it, and then goes on to fondle them long after they are dead. Just so, it is possible for us to smother whatever vitality our religious faith may have by holding to its forms too rigidly and then with little or no awareness continuing to fondle that from which the spirit has fled.

In conclusion, let me suggest the possibility of a similar peril to our nation. The one thing about her that we esteem above all else is her heritage of freedom. This we would insure to our children and our children's children. But unless our methods of insuring freedom are also freedom's methods, there is not only the grave but the almost certain risk of losing what we would insure. Eternal vigilance is still the price of liberty, but it should be vigilant enough to avoid crushing liberty in the very process of defending it.

In all our approaches to life—whether toward friends and loved ones, our work, our country, or our religion, there are few of us who do not need to be on guard against unconscious impulses to destroy the very thing we treasure. And some of us need to be on guard constantly.[61]

CHAPTER 14

HAPPINESS DEPENDS ON THE DENOMINATOR OF DESIRE

In the second paragraph of the Declaration of Independence we read these words. "We hold these truths to be self-evident, that all men are created equal, that they are endowed by their creator with certain unalienable rights, that among these are life, liberty and the pursuit of happiness."

You will note that it is not the right to happiness but only the right to pursue it that is classed along with the rights of life and liberty. It cannot be denied that while most of us are engaged in a rather frantic pursuit, too many of us never find very much happiness. For, what is happiness?

First, let us consider what it is not. I think you will agree that pleasure is not a synonym for happiness. Nor is happiness the sum of our pleasures. Nor do all our pleasures necessarily contribute to whatever measure of happiness we may be able to achieve. For example, you and I may take genuine pleasure in losing our temper on occasion, experiencing a real thrill in giving free vent to our instinct for aggressiveness. Surely, a pleasant feeling arises within us from this uninhibited assertion of our own egos. But in all likelihood, a loss of temper will not bring us happiness. Quite the contrary! It may result in a long aftermath of spiritual depression.

Pleasure is an effervescent thing. It consists of a temporary gratification of an impulse or a taste. Some pleasures are worthy, some unworthy, and some are vicious. But happiness is an experience far more lasting and far more fundamental than pleasure. Happiness consists of an abiding satisfaction that has its source in a sense of interior harmony. It is not something that can be pursued directly and achieved by that pursuit, but nearly always comes as a result of something else. It is like the smooth running of a huge driving wheel in a machine shop that turns all the other machines. When it is turning on its axis, there is scarcely any noise at all. This is a sign that all the parts of the wheel are in balance, and that all internal stresses and strains have been reduced to a minimum. And so it is with ourselves. Happiness is the result of something else already achieved. It means that the machinery of our lives is running smoothly, that there is an absence of inward friction because the forces in our lives are in balance. How many of us are happy in this sense?

Not too long ago while riding on one of our public conveyances I was struck by the tenseness of the faces of the people in the conveyance,—very sober and serious, many of them looked anxious. Very few countenances were radiant with inward joy. And yet, what are we here for? What is the purpose of life? Are we to ride back and forth from one place to another and not enjoy the ride? The old catechism says: "We are here to praise God and enjoy Him forever." Enjoyment, happiness may not be the purpose of life, but it certainly is evidence that the major purpose is being served. Now both Buddha and Jesus spoke of blessedness (or happiness—if you will) as the result of something else. They did not regard it as something to be pursued and achieved directly. Certain conditions are required before happiness comes. "Blessed are they who hunger and thirst after righteousness," said Jesus. "To abhor and cease from evil, not to be weary in well-doing, this is the greatest blessing," said Buddha. "Blessed are the peacemakers, for they shall be called the children of God," said Jesus. Buddha says, "Associate with the peaceable, be long-suffering and meek, this is the greatest blessing," and so forth. It is in this high sense in which Jesus and Buddha used the words "blessing," that I would use the word "happy."

Of how many of us can it be said that we are living a happy and blessed existence? "Hope springs eternal in the human breast. Man never is, but always to be blessed." And yet the time to be blessed is now, the hour of happiness is the present hour. How many men and women cheat themselves by promising themselves a felicity that is going to take place in the future or permit themselves to sigh for some paradise lost? They do not allow the machinery of their lives to function smoothly. It is put out of balance by their worrying about the past or the future or magnifying the difficulties of the present.

I wonder how many of you know the story about "The Two Doors"? I read it sometime ago in the *Christian Century*. It is the story of a dream a certain man had as he slept at night. He saw a vast hall down which row upon row of men and women of all nationalities were advancing, and at the end of the hall were two doors. Over one door was the inscription: "This way to Heaven," and over the other door "This way to a lecture on heaven," and the whole company went through the door to the lecture on heaven. The implications of the story are very simple yet profound. In these modern times many of us are in danger of missing the real, firsthand experiences of life through our own preoccupation with them as problems. Instead of reading a poem, we read a criticism of it. Instead of wandering through the country-side and enjoying its beauty at first-hand, we listen to others tell of the beauty of the country-side. We allow ourselves to become absorbed in thinking about the significance of something which some day, not now, is going to be ours. We go to the lecture about heaven, when we might enter into heaven itself. In other words, most of us do what I am doing now: we make a problem of happiness instead of embracing it.

Let me repeat, the time to be happy is now, the place to be happy is right where we are. How many of us go through life constantly deluding ourselves by the thought that if we only had a different environment we could then settle down to a blessed existence. If we live in the city, we deram of what bliss it would be to have a little home in the country. And if we live in the country, we dream of the luxury and convenience of living in a cozy cramped-up apartment. I wonder if you saw that cartoon of the fireman in one of the newspapers recently. There were two pictures of the fireman. In one the fireman was counting the months and the days until he would be able to retire from his job of putting out fires, counting the days until he would be able to move to the country and have a nice chicken farm. And then you have a second picture of him a year after he has retired, and he is back in the fire-engine house, once more talking to the men about the "good old days when they had real fires." If we only had a change of scenery, a new kind of employment, a new set of friends, happiness would be ours! Perhaps so, and perhaps not. It all depends upon the inward state of our minds. It would certainly be untrue to human experience to deny that a change of environment has wrought wonders in the contentment of some people. But it would be equally untrue to human experience to deny that for others the change of environment would make no difference whatsoever. They would not know happiness no matter where they went because they have not learned that the kingdom of heaven which is the kingdom of blessedness is primarily within themselves.

Now most of the great seers of mankind, most of the major prophets have pointed out this fact. Buddha has put it into a mathematical formula: Happiness is equal to what we have divided by what we desire. As you examine the writings of Buddha you will not find these exact words, but that is the substance of what he must have had in mind. If we write our equation "H" for happiness, "P" for possessions and "D" for desire

$$\text{Then } H = \frac{P}{D}^{62}$$

If we have something and desire nothing, then we can be supremely happy, because mathematically we know that something divided by nothing is infinity. But if we always desire something more, no matter how much we may have, then our happiness is a fraction. No matter how big the numerator of possessions is if the denominator of desire is constantly expanding, then the resulting happiness must approach zero, because any number divided by infinity is nothing.

You see we must keep the denominator of desire at least equal to or less than the numerator of acquisition if we would know something more than a fragmentary happiness. If we could expand the numerator without expanding the denominator, we should be making progress. But, the strange paradox about the mathematics of happiness is this: That when we attempt to increase what we have, we are most likely to increase *what we want*, a great deal more. That was the fundamental discovery that Buddha made. Now I am convinced that he has called our attention to a profound truth. It may not be the whole truth, but I believe it is a vital and important aspect of truth.

If we would know inward blessedness we must pay some attention to this denominator of desire. Now I know that for Western people it is going to be hard to comprehend this idea. It is going to sound to them like nonsense. But if we let our wishes run away with us, if we let our ambitions greatly outstrip our abilities and our yearnings leave our opportunities behind, then a tension will be set up in our lives and we shall become aware of unbearable stress and strains.

We must learn to keep our wants, our wishes, within reasonable bounds. Buddha would have us banish them to the vanishing point, but we of the Occident are not prepared to go as far as he would wish us to go. There is no chance of that and no danger. There is no danger because all of the propaganda and advertising that comes by way of the radio, the television, our newspapers and magazines is calculated to make us want ever and ever more things. We seldom hear anybody say: "Why don't you get along on a little less?" No, that is not the propaganda which we hear today. But unless we heed Buddha's advice and pay some attention to this factor of coveting and yearning for more things, we are bound to fall short of knowing the greatest blessings of life.

Now what are some of the things men desire, the attainment of which leaves them unhappy because they are encouraged thereby to keep on wanting ever more and more?

First and foremost, both Jesus and Buddha maintained that material possessions do not necessarily make us happy. The acquisition of this world's goods becomes with some

114

people a veritable disease. They can not rest content with what they have but must be forever straining to add to their store. The more they get, the more they want. They long to lay their hands on things, and gadgets and conveniences, "building ever bigger and bigger barns," as Jesus phrased it, "gaining the whole world, and losing their own souls." Possession becomes obsession. We know people who when they have safely laid aside enough to take care of their present and future needs, continue to stretch out their hands for more and yet never find the blessed state of mind which is the unconscious motive behind their pursuit. Thank heaven, the rank and file of men and women know when and how to limit their desires in this direction to their needs. If it were not so, the mad scramble to keep up with the Joneses would be much madder than it now is.

The recognition of our fellowman is another thing that men desire which makes some people always miserable because no matter how much recognition they receive, they feel they never get enough. Now, it is entirely natural for all of us to covet some form of recognition from our fellow men, but there are those who do not know when to be satisfied. They must be forever pushing themselves forward, climbing the social ladder, proclaiming their honors from the housetops. They want to be known favorably—but above all, they want to be known. They cannot tolerate being one among the many. Not to stand out from the crowd is to feel neglected. To sense that one is the object of the public eye must be a thrilling experience, but to make it the condition of one's own felicity is to insure one's disappointment and disillusionment in the long run. For there is nothing that is quite so fickle as the attention of the public. Today we may be somebody, but tomorrow we may easily find ourselves nobody in particular. Thank heaven, the great mass of people are fairly sensible about disciplining their desires in the direction of publicity and notoriety. If everyone struggled frantically to stand out from the crowd there would not be much of a crowd to stand out from. The competition would be terrible, no one would have any peace of mind. To become a publicity hound is literally to be cursed.

Still another danger to the happiness of man is the craving for power. There are those who do not care who gets the credit, who gets the applause or recognition so long as they can pull the strings behind the scenes. They like to feel that people and events are under their control. They thrill to the thought of dominating others. The love of power, however, has a tendency to become a lust—to become an insatiable appetite, a devastating, ungovernable desire. We are told the story of Alexander the Great, how when he had conquered the world he sat down and sighed because there were no more worlds to conquer. Whether that be a true story or not, it is certainly true that there are enough instances in life to show that when some men are permitted to exercise a little power, their heads are turned and they are made miserable by the yearning to exercise a greater power for which they have no capacity. "Man, proud man," says Shakespeare, "drest in a little brief authority, most ignorant of what he's most assured. . . . plays such fantastic tricks before high heaven as makes the angels weep." [63] And the most fantastic trick of all is to rob himself of inward harmony by permitting himself to strain after something far beyond his grasp. To limit one's desire for power is one of the ways to be happy.

But of course, the surest way, the way described by Buddha and Jesus is to serve others and to share what we have with them. In this most of the great seers and prophets are agreed. To curb our own desires by a deliberate act of the will is a very difficult thing to do, but as the getting of more things tends to increase our desires, so when we share what we have with those less fortunate than ourselves, we have a tendency to reduce further the denominator of our own desire.

The poet has summed it up in these words:

For we must share if we would keep,
That blessing from above:
Ceasing to give, we cease to have,—
Such is the law of love.[64]

116

But even here we must be on our guard lest the impulse to serve others becomes a new and even more tyrannical longing, outstripping all reasonable possibility of fulfillment. For there are people who add to the total misery of the world by making themselves miserable worrying too much about what they would like to do for others and cannot do. To yearn to render a service far beyond our own capacity or opportunity to render, can unbalance the minds of the best, as much as any other stress and strain. And I am thinking especially about certain parents I have known who are ready to make almost any sacrifice in behalf of their children, but who covet so much for them, far beyond their own power to provide, that they in turn are so empty and impoverished in their own personalities that they are scarcely fit companions for their children. Even the desire to serve others must be disciplined by reason. There is no substitute for sound judgment. For no matter how fast or how far we may increase the numerator of achievement, if we increase the denominator of desire even faster and farther, including even the desire to serve others, we are bound to know only a fractional fulfillment of life. We are doomed to disillusionment.

Now the religion that finds its center in India and in Buddhist China has been engaged for centuries in increasing the happiness of the world by whittling down the denominator of desire, while we in the West, in spite of our religion —in spite of the religion at least of Jesus, have been increasing the numerator of acquisition and achievement. Our genius has gone in this direction. Perhaps the real truth lies somewhere between these two concepts. I think, however, we in America could learn something from the Orient about looking after this denominator of desire, while they in turn could learn something from us about the numerator of achievement. Here we are constantly being urged to become dissatisfied with what we already have and to reach out for what the Joneses have. From almost every direction we are being made aware of the things money can buy while less and less stress is being made on the things money can not buy. Possession of things has become almost an obsession with us. The sin of covetousnes has been exalted into almost a virtue and yet if our way of life is destined eventually to be destroyed from within it will more than likely be from our increasing and unashamed covetousness.

A French philosopher, Francois La Rochefoucauld, who lived three centuries ago, speaks to us today more pertinently than he did to his own generation when he said—

> Few things are needful to make the wise man happy but nothing satisfies the fool; and this is the reason why so many of mankind are miserable.[65]

Yes, there are those who are miserable because they have too little, but there are also those who are miserable because they have too much and still want more.

CHAPTER 15

TO GROW UP IS TO PUT AWAY CHILDISH THINGS

Not long ago I happened one day to observe a man trying to jack up the back wheel of his automobile in order to put on a tire. After two or three unsuccessful attempts to get the jack to work, the man lost his temper and with a blast of profanity he gave the jack a sudden boot, and from the look on his face, one would gather that he had injured his foot more than he had injured the jack. He must have been a man about forty years of age, but surely he was acting like a two-year-old. Surely one of the main causes of much of the personal frustration and unhappiness of adults today lies in the fact that in growing up to manhood and womanhood in a physical way, many of us have neglected to grow up in our emotions and understanding. We have left behind us the physical bodies of our childhood but not all our childish attitudes and habits. In short, many of us are afflicted with what has come to be called "adult infantilism."

After many years of experience which has permitted me to enter more or less intimately in the lives of many people, I am convinced that emotional immaturity on the part of adults wrecks more marriages, breaks up more homes, ruins more careers than any other single factor. Psychologists are telling us that adult infantilism is our chief deficiency as a people, our most conspicuous national shortcoming; that it is responsible for more social maladjustment, more family discord, more intellectual vagrancy, more real unhappiness than any disease, derangement or other disharmony of modern life. And the number of people thus afflicted seems to be increasing. As I understand it, the average Chinaman is much more mature emotionally than the average American. Adult

119

infantilism as defined by the psychologists is the condition and conduct of an individual who, having reached the maturity of physical development and it may be even intellectual development still remains infantile in his response to the demands and obligations of life. How many today can confidently say with the Apostle Paul, "When I was a child I spake as a child, I understood as a child, I thought as a child, but when I became a man, I put away childish things?" [66] Many, it is true, have succeeded in putting away the superficial things of childhood, while unconsciously retaining its fundamental traits and behavior patterns. Thus the ranks of arrested development are being recruited by men and women who are physically and chronologically adults, but spiritually and psychologically still little children. At a certain point in their education they simply stopped growing up. Their minds have graduated from grammar and high school and even college, but their emotions did not even graduate from the kindergarten.

How comforting it is to know that there are probably very few who have completely put away all childish ways of feeling and behaving! But, to take comfort in such knowledge, as someone has pointed out, is in itself one of the signs of immaturity, for the fully mature person spurns the consolation to be derived from considering the prevalence of shortcomings similar to his own. It is certainly a childish trait to be satisfied by comparing ourselves with the average. We have grown up only when we are inclined to compare ourselves with our own potential best. Now, there are many more obvious signs of maturity than this.

For instance, the mature person endeavors at all times to take full responsibility for his own mistakes and failures. I think it was the first Henry Ford who observed, or is credited with this observation. In describing a certain individual he said, "He met misfortune like a man. He blamed it on his wife." It is a sure sign of arrested development when one invariably blames others for his own shortcomings. And yet there are men who are constantly excusing their lack of success either on their business associates or their wives, and women attributing their unhappiness either to their husbands or to other relatives, and both men and women blaming their parents or their early environment for misfortunes of their own making. They meet with a preventable accident, they lose their positions because of a show of temper, they make a bad investment, or they exercise poor judgment in a hundred different ways. How convenient it is to place the blame on someone else, but also how infantile, and how futile. Now, somewhere in somebody's office I have seen the motto, a motto which should be shouted from the housetops, and whispered into the ear at midnight: "A man can fail many times, but he isn't a failure until he begins to blame somebody else." Here we have in a nutshell a formula by which one can appraise his own emotional development. A child is reluctant to face uncomfortable knowledge about himself and is quick to offer excuses. The mature person is reluctant to shirk or even share the blame for mistakes that he knows are largely his own.

Again, a sure sign of maturity is freedom from dependence upon praise and gratitude as motivations in life. The spiritually adult person may enjoy the plaudits of his friends whenever they are forthcoming, but they are not essential to his peace of mind or to the vigor of his life. He has long since ceased to regard genuine gratitude as anything but one of the most uncertain rewards of life. He is wise enough to know that to expect it is to diminish its probability, and to demand it is well nigh to destroy its possibility. He therefore counts it as one of the illusive, unpredictable windfalls of life. Whenever he does his duty, he does it for the immediate personal satisfaction of having done his duty. If he goes further and does the generous thing, it is likewise for the immediate satisfaction of expressing the generous side of his own nature. It is the mark of a childish mind to be unduly disturbed by the small amount of appreciation and recognition which one receives in life. A grown-up person does not have to have his virtues and good deeds praised in order to feel that life is worth living.

Again, he who has reached true maturity does not have to run things in order to be interested in them. When a little child refuses to take part in a given game after he

121

has ceased to be "it" or to pout on the sidelines when he cannot have his own way, we easily recognize this as a childish attitude of mind. "I won't play." But when we, as men and women, lose our enthusiasm for some club or church or organization or political party or worthwhile cause of any kind, almost immediately after having surrendered some strategic office in the club or church, we do not recognize so easily the same childish trait in ourselves. A reluctance to cooperate in some enterprise when others are given the leadership that we once possessed is an unmistakable evidence of arrested development.

Jesus must have had this type in mind when he rebuked the indifference of the Scribes and Pharisees to both his own mission and that of John the Baptist. John the Baptist proclaimed the Kingdom of God in terms of wrath, Jesus in terms of love. One came fasting, playing the funeral march of a dying order, the other came feasting, playing the wedding march of the new order to be. But both Jesus and John the Baptist met with little cooperation from the religious leaders of their day. "Whereunto shall I liken the men of this generation?" said Jesus, "They are like little children that sit in the market place and call to one another, saying: 'We piped unto you and you did not dance, we wailed and ye did not weep,'" we played at giving a wedding party and at conducting a funeral service but in neither case would you Scribes and Pharisees lend any cooperation. It is a sign of maturity when one can let others do the piping without losing one's interest in the dance, or can surrender the leadership in wailing without refusing to play an inconspicuous role of merely being one of the mourners. In short, no one has truly grown up emotionally and spiritually who cannot see himself superceded in any office and still be vitally interested in the cause which that office subserves, provided of course, the cause is still considered to be as worthy as before.

Now, there are other signs of maturity. For instance, the mature person can explain his real convictions on almost any subject, whether it be on religion or politics or on how to bring up children without losing his temper. His voice may rise in volume with the excitement of the debate, but it will not rise in venom. He knows how to keep his temper under control. He has learned how to differ with others in opinions and judgments without arousing their emotions and their resentments. I have never been to China, but as I understand it, it is generally conceded over there that in any argument between two persons the first to get angry has lost the argument, even when he did not need to do so. The Chinese have put away many childish things, not all of them, of course, maybe not even half of them. I do not know the percentage, but I understand that they have put away this temptation to go into temper tantrums in an argument in order to get their own way.

Still another sign of maturity is the capacity to take frustrations and misfortunes in stride. The emotional adult does not cry too hard over "spilt milk" or bewail too long over a broken doll. To indulge in vain regrets, to chastise oneself mentally for some neglected opportunity in the past or mistaken judgment, to refuse to forgive oneself for sins of which one has fully repented, is not only a waste of precious energy, it is evidence of a retarded awareness of life. The mature person does not "cry for the moon," he knows enough to limit his ambitions to the realities of life. He understands the value of a goal that is beyond his immediate grasp, even the value of a receding goal that continually lures him on, but he does not refuse to take the first mile because he cannot see beyond the bend in the road to the second one. He does not refuse the better because he cannot as yet achieve the best. He accepts the half loaf when he cannot get the whole loaf. He takes satisfactions in seeing his ideals even partially realized.

Finally, just as there is such a thing as emotional immaturity, so there is such a thing as religious immaturity, a stage of arrested development which may be described as the religion of the nursery and the kindergarten. As a matter of fact, the remarks of the Apostle Paul about putting away childish things is in that thirteenth chapter of First Corinthians where he is discussing the essence of religion. What is religion? "And now abideth faith, hope, love, these

123

three, but the greatest of these is love." A child is likely to reach after the tinsels of life, the gaudy toy, the glittering object, and not consider real worth and substance and so the childish mind in regard to religion is likely to consider the superficialities, the pageantry, and the glitter of religion as the real thing and overlook the inner life, which as Paul says, is the life of "faith, hope, and love."

Furthermore, the childish mind in religion is readily impressed by fairy tales and fables. It has not learned to distinguish between fact on the one hand and fiction on the other. It has not learned to differentiate between truth and authority. It is just as likely as not to take authority for truth and more than likely to mistake *a* truth for *the* truth. Whereas the religiously mature person is acquainted with all these distinctions and does not identify fact with fiction nor accept mere authority for truth, nor is he likely to believe that one individual of any one religion possesses the truth, the whole truth, and nothing but the truth.

The adult is concerned with the substance and inner worth of religion. The childish mind attributes holiness to times, places and things. The mature mind finds holiness only in motives and purposes, in ideas and ideals. The one confronts the darkness of the unknown in fear and trembling, but the other knows that the universe is his home, and therefore does not fear the unknown. The one is naïve enough to hope for and even to expect uninterrupted peace and joy, the other understands that there are such things as tides of the spirit, which sometimes leave the soul stranded on the shoals, but eventually return as swelling floods to search him out and bear him farther on. In short, the childish person is inclined to look upon heaven and hell as exterior realities, whereas the mature person in religion is inclined to believe that heaven and hell are within the human soul.

These then are some of the signs of maturity as I see it. How many of us fall short of full adulthood, how many of us from time to time give evidence of arrested development? The part of wisdom is not to test our friends and neighbors but to make a faithful examination of our own selves. For he who is even partially aware of his own infantile feelings

124

and behavior patterns, is already well on the way to reaching the position where he can truthfully say, "When I was a child, I spake as a child, I understood as a child, I thought as a child, but when I became a man, when I became a woman, and especially when I became a parent, I put away childish things."

CHAPTER 16

EVIL CAN BE OVERCOME ONLY BY GOOD

In our attempt to stress the affirmative rather than the negative aspects of faith, this chapter is no exception in spite of the fact that we declare that evil cannot be overcome by evil. For the same theme may be stated in positive terms as we affirm that evil can be overcome only by good.

From ancient times down to the present men of good will among all creeds and races have been confronted by the presence of evil in the world and have sought to overcome it in various ways. Men of good will have been united in their condemnation of such obvious evils, for example, as theft, dishonesty, vice, murder, cruelty, and tyranny. In addition, evils that once were scarcely recognized as such have, down through the centuries, come to be classed as evils by an ever-increasing number of people; such evils, for example, as slavery, the duel, cruelty to animals, racial discrimination, and now at last aggressive war. Where men of good will have differed widely is in the means employed to overcome evil, some taking the position that "the end justifies the means," have been willing to employ almost any means available.

And here precisely is where the liberal parts company with his non-liberal friends. The liberal has historically repudiated the doctrine that the end justifies the means. For he holds that the means we employ in fighting evil must be consistent with the end we seek to serve—that the values we expect in the goal must first appear in the methods we use to reach it. In short, that it is utter folly to believe that evil can be overcome by evil or that moral purposes can be served by unethical procedures. Six hundred years before Christ the distinguished Chinese philosopher Laotze declared,

"I would return good for good, I would also return good for evil. I would meet trust with trust. I would likewise meet suspicion with confidence." [66a] Five hundred years before Jesus the founder of Buddhism formulated the liberal point of view on this question in these words: "Never does hatred cease by hatred here below; hatred ceases by love. This is the eternal law." [66b] Jesus himself expressed essentially the same idea when he inquired, "How can Satan cast out Satan? If a kingdom is divided against itself, that kingdom cannot stand." [67] The Apostle Paul said, "Be not overcome by evil but overcome evil by good." [68] In modern times the liberal point of view may be put in these words, "The means we employ constitute the only end we are ever likely to realize."

Now men of good will have seen rather clearly that in certain instances at least it is indeed utter folly to fight evil with evil. For example, what father would expect to overcome the use of profanity in his son by swearing at him? What mother could hope to reform successfully the habit of lying in her daughter by setting her an example of prevarication? And what teacher would presume to correct the use of poor English on the part of a pupil by phrasing her rebuke in the most recent slang? And yet when it comes to such evils as anger, hatred, suspicion, fear, arrogance, we are often tempted to fight anger with anger, hatred with hatred, fear with fear, arrogance with arrogance, resentment with resentment with the result that instead of overcoming these evils in others, we merely succeed in permitting these evils to conquer ourselves. How often we all have found this to be true in our own lives, and to our own sorrow!

Now one of the most persistent delusions of the human race is the false promise that the use of violence offers for the solution of its problems. From earliest times down to the present, violence has constantly appealed to the human imagination as a short cut to liberty, justice, peace, and security. And this in spite of the glaring fact that by and large violence has generally proved to be the longest way round to whatever goal mankind has sought to reach. Now the reformer and the social revolutionist in all centuries have been peculiarly prone to this delusion. Beholding some specific injustice they are resolved to get rid of it, and then on the other hand they note the inertia, the indifference of the common people, and becoming discouraged with the slow and tedious work of persuading the world to accept their ideas and plans, they turn with a sigh of relief to the use of force and direct action as offering the quickest method of obtaining their objectives. Thus the world has again and again been needlessly deluged in blood and civil strife, while smoothly working economies have been turned into chaos and bankruptcy. Wholly unnecessary rebellions and revolutions have been precipitated in this world by utterly sincere but fanatically obsessed, impatient men. The goals they sought were good, but the methods they employed were self-defeating. For the resort to violence is invariably followed by a period of reaction and the progress of mankind in the end found to be not accelerated but retarded instead.

For example, it is easy now to see in retrospect that the issues of the French revolution and the American civil war, just to mention two illustrations, could have been settled more cheaply, more satisfactorily, more efficiently for all concerned without resort to arms as M. Turgot, minister of Finance under the French monarchy, advised in the first instance, and as Senator Henry Clay, the great statesman from Kentucky, advised in the second. Now the basic issue at stake in the French revolution was land monopoly. The masses of the people could not get access to the land. So M. Turgot suggested that the French monarchy should purchase some of the huge estates of the nobility and clergy and rent these out at reasonable rates to the people. But there were dunderheads in those days, as in other days, who thought the expense was simply exorbitant, the whole idea was absurd, the nation could not afford it, it would put the country in bankruptcy. And so the advice of M. Turgot was ignored, but the revolution and the reign of terror which followed confiscated the lands of the nobility which cost ten to twenty times the puny sum suggested by this wise statesman, and it also cost the monarchy its life, its very existence.

Before the civil war came, Senator Henry Clay of Kentucky foresaw what was coming. He saw how the issue of Negro slavery was dividing the North and the South into two hostile camps which were bound to fight it out sooner or later unless something intervened. Therefore, he sponsored a bill in Congress to authorize the government to purchase all Negro slaves from their masters and set them free. Four billions of dollars was the amount which he calculated to be necessary. But there were dunderheads in those days too, who threw up their hands in ghastly horror at his suggestion. The nation could not afford the expense, it would put us in bankruptcy. On the other hand there were those who argued the slave-owners ought not be paid a cent for they had no business to purchase slaves in the first place; it was pure blackmail. So the South opposed it, and the abolitionists in the North opposed it. Each thought he was absolutely right and refused to compromise or to see the vision of Henry Clay. The result was the resort to arms and violence. And then this nation paid many times over the four billion dollars originally suggested by Henry Clay; and in addition, not only killed off thousands and hundreds of thousands of its most able bodied citizens, but sowed so much hatred and bitterness that its harvest of vengeance is still being reaped. For the full emancipation of the Negro is not only unachieved today, but it is not even yet in sight. There are people in the South and in the North that are still fighting the civil war because of the great legacy of bitterness which that war left us.

Now Great Britain, on the other hand, accomplished the complete abolition of Negro slavery throughout her dominions without resort to bloodshed and violence and therefore without any legacy of hatred to plague her subsequent political life. There have been some recent race riots in London, but you note that they have almost completely subsided. Why? There is no public opinion to support such extravagance. That is why the government is able to keep this violence at a minimum. There is no legacy of hatred to disturb and complicate their problem of race relations.

Now let there be no misunderstanding of the liberal position concerning the relation of means to an end. The liberal is not dogmatically opposed to all use of force. He is

129

not necessarily a non-resistant. For he will defend his loved ones and his country against all acts of physical violence. No, he is not opposed to the use of force under the sanctions of law. On the contrary, he accepts it as a moral means of holding evil in check. He understands that a certain measure of force is absolutely necessary as a solution to most of society's problems, principally as a restraint to protect society against the aggressiveness of individuals or groups. But his preferred method is persuasion rather than coercion. He points to the fact that there are large areas of human relations which do not respond to compulsions of any kind. One may restrain the evil man from injuring his fellow man, but it is never possible to make the evil man good or the good man better, except by arousing the dormant divinity within him. This calls for persuasion, for education, for the inspiration of example. And without doubt this is the largest area of life. Here voluntary cooperation is absolutely necessary and nothing else can be relied upon to take its place. It has been called "the area of obedience to the unenforceable."

What is required is the transformation of impulses and attitudes, the reformation of people's ways of thinking and feeling. It is precisely here where the liberal can function most effectively. And it is also precisely here that the liberal faces his greatest danger. Simply because these hidden attitudes and emotions of men are most stubborn in their resistance to change, the reformer is tempted to overcome evil by another evil, to cast out Satan by employing the very methods of Satan. If the evil forces he would combat use smearing tactics, dishonest propaganda, innuendo, and lurid appeals to ulterior motives, he is tempted to fight fire with fire, and thus take on the very vices he would overcome in others.

To illustrate how subtle and yet how powerful is this temptation, it is only necessary to point out how much of the spirit of Communism we have already acquired in fighting the evil in Communism. Now one of the practices of the Communists we have most vigorously condemned is their ruthless suppression of minority opinion in their midst. And yet here we are in democratic America, recently having adopted tactics and procedures that jeopardize the civil liberties of all patriotic American citizens in order to get at the comparatively few subversives in our midst. Let us be grateful that the worst excesses of McCarthyism are behind us. Let us be grateful that the common sense of the American people has triumphed and that the judges of our supreme court have had the courage and the wisdom to keep us from wrecking our Bill of Rights. Even so the spirit of McCarthyism is not entirely dead. It will not completely subside so long as this East and West struggle continues. An emergency may arise when the spirit of McCarthyism may come to the fore once more to imperil the basic rights of all our citizens.

Again we have condemned, have we not, the Communists that wherever they get into power they set up a police state, and lay great stress on their secret agents. And yet we here in America have increasingly imitated their practice in this respect and have developed our own secret service to a point where the number engaged in it has reached an all time high. Let us thank the American people and the judges of our supreme court that our police state cannot act as arbitrarily and as ruthlessly as that in the Soviet Union.

Again we have condemned, have we not, the Communists because of their chauvinistic boasting before the world of their own scientific and military achievements. And how do we combat them? By making similar boastings before the world.

We have condemned the Communists because they threaten to pollute the world's atmosphere with renewed testing of nuclear weapons. And how do we fight them? By threatening to pollute the world's atmosphere with our own renewed testing of nuclear weapons. It is tit for tat; it is boast for boast; it is threat for threat; reprisal for reprisal. And so the war of nerves goes on from bad to worse. Until one side or the other has the imagination and the statesmanship to employ some other tactics, there will be no sound solution for the present East-West struggle.

Surely we do not expect to overcome the evils of war by going to war. The solution lies not in coercion but in conciliation. We should resort not to more violence and blood

131

but to reason and voluntary cooperation and more diplomacy, not to fear and hatred, but to good faith and good will. We cannot achieve our own security without first achieving the security of all mankind. It seems to me this should be almost elementary in our consideration. Arbitration, reasonable compromise, the spirit of accommodation, placing our trust in more law and order, this is the attitude which has held our nation together in the past and has made us a great people, and this in my judgment is the only attitude which is going to solve our internal problem of racial discrimination; this is the only attitude which is going to solve our external problem of achieving a durable peace between the East and the West. If we continue our present obsession, meeting arrogance with arrogance, stubbornness with stubbornness, violence with violence, intolerance with intolerance, and recrimination with recrimination, we may end up by destroying ourselves before we have even had a chance to destroy our enemy. Because in fighting them in this way we are bound to take on their worst vices.

In our own day Mahatma Gandhi has given us a superb example of how to overcome evil, a superb, practical example, namely, by employing only the weapons of good will and good faith. Gandhi himself renounced all violence, he refused even to employ any secret agents in his cause, everything had to be out in the open and above board. He refused to countenance any form of repression within his own ranks. Almost single handed he achieved one of the greatest triumphs ever recorded in history. He won independence for his people with a minimum loss of life and property. Whatever blunders that took place were committed by his less loyal followers who were unable to rise to the level of his statesmanship. Even so the legacy of bitterness which that revolution has left behind in India, is almost insignificant in comparison to that left behind in most revolutions in history.

There is a man in this country, a distinguished Negro minister by the name of Dr. Martin Luther King, who is in the very process of demonstrating the effectiveness, the practicability of Gandhi's tactics in our very nation. It is not too early to say to date that he has at least achieved a partial triumph. Of course, much remains to be done to obtain first-class citizenship for all our colored fellow Americans, but if this problem is to be solved effectively, I believe that the spirit that animates Dr. Martin Luther King, plus intelligent application of the supreme court's recent decision on the race issue, is the only way to follow. There is a minimum of restraining force that must be used in the solution of almost every problem, but let it be kept thus and not exceeded. What we should all learn to do is to put our maximum stress upon education, upon persuasion, and upon the inspiration of example. Herein lies the secret of solving our internal problems and our external problems, of rooting out evil. While there is yet time, let us realize the utter folly of fighting evil with evil and renounce all such self-defeating methods in so far as it is humanly possible to do so. Evil cannot be overcome by evil, but evil can be overcome by good.

CHAPTER 17

INDIVIDUALS, NOT INSTITUTIONS HAVE RIGHTS

Individuals, not institutions have rights. Whatever rights institutions may be accorded are derived from the individuals they are organized to serve. It is the individual who possesses inalienable rights, because he has been made in the image of that which is infinite and eternal. This is one of the major premises upon which the liberal bases his whole philosophy of life. We can not prove it; it is not anything that can be proven. It is an axiom that we assume, and our faith in it gives it substance. It becomes a rock. When we lose our faith in it, it becomes shifting sand; and that which has been built upon it crumbles. Let us not forget that our liberal movement, historically speaking, began as a mighty protest against the Calvinistic doctrine of the depravity of man. John Calvin of Geneva held that man is a degenerate child of God, an angel fallen from grace, and has become a worm in the dust, so to speak, without any merits of his own.

Now over two centuries ago liberals in this country, in Great Britain and elsewhere, challenged this concept of John Calvin; they proclaimed the very opposite, namely, the essential dignity of man, insisting upon his innate divinity and his potential capacity for progressive development. Today the question of man's infinite worth before God is no longer very much of a controversial issue, certainly not in intellectual circles, and I believe only mildly so among the masses of the people.

A much more important division, however, has arisen over man's relation to the institutions of human society. Which comes first? The welfare of man or the welfare of his institutions? Which has priority? This is where the liberal begins to part company with his non-liberal friends. For the thorough-going liberal has always proclaimed the priority of man over all institutions of society.

To illustrate what he means, he goes back to Jesus of Nazareth; not because Jesus is necessarily the last word on all questions, but because Jesus has on this particular question expressed more clearly and cogently the liberal position than anyone else. I refer to what he said about the Sabbath, one of the great institutions of his day and of our own day. He said the Sabbath was made for man, not man for the Sabbath. In his day the Sabbath had become something of a hardship. For example, it was illegal for neighbors to visit one another on that day, to do any kind of work, to go anywhere except to the synagogue, to pick grain from the fields even if one were hungry, or allay the suffering of the sick in an emergency. Now Jesus thought this to be an absurd, unreasonable state of affairs, a complete reversal of what ought to be, a travesty on the original purpose for which the Sabbath had been deliberately ordained. Instead of a blessing it had become a burden, instead of a servant of man it had become a tyrant over him; instead of a means to a good end, it had become an end in itself. Now Jesus had no intention to abolish the Sabbath day or even to make light of it. His purpose was to restore it as a day of rest and gladness. He somehow felt it was made for man and not man for it, and in this feeling he was not only true to his deepest instincts, but he was true to ancient scripture as well.

The observance of one day in seven is an ancient institution. The children of Israel took it over from the cult of moon worshippers who had observed the Sabbath long before there were any children of Israel. The time of the new moon, the full moon, and the first and last quarters had long been celebrated by appropriate feasts and religious ceremonies throughout the whole region of the Mediterranean Sea. So when the prophets of Israel came along, noting what a boon the observance of one day in seven was to tired slaves and to workmen in general, they incorporated the Sabbath into the religion of Israel; but they did it for humanitarian reasons. In the book of Deuteronomy they wrote, "Remember that thou wast a servant in the land of Egypt, and that the

135

Lord thy God brought thee out thence through a mighty hand and by an outstretched arm; therefore the Lord thy God commanded thee to keep the Sabbath day." [69] It was a day meant for slaves, people who had been tired, a day of rest and gladness, but the priests who followed the prophets, insisted upon the observance of the Sabbath for entirely different reasons. They were not primarily interested in the Sabbath as a day of rest for tired workers; they were interested in it as an occasion for the calling of assemblies and the solemn meeting. Their point of view was expressed in the book of Exodus, where the priest explained how the Sabbath was instituted as a holy ordinance. "In six days the Lord made heaven and earth, the sea, and all that in them is, and rested the seventh day. Wherefore the Lord blessed the Sabbath day and hallowed it." [70] Because God rested on the Sabbath day and blessed it, therefore the day is to be observed as a holy day, a time sacred in itself, not merely as a means to a humanitarian end.

What a difference there is between the institutionalist on the one hand and the humanitarian on the other, between the priestly and prophetic points of view on this issue! And this vast gulf in attitude holds true so far as all the other ordinances, customs and institutions of mankind. The true liberal in every age makes bold to declare that the priority of man must be maintained not only over the Sabbath but also over all other institutions of human society.

Now let us consider the application of this principle to such institutions, for example, as the church, free enterprise, labor unions, and finally government. We will discuss these very briefly.

First of all the church. What is the church for? Is it an end in itself? How shall it be regarded? Designed originally as an instrument for man's spiritual welfare, as an agency to advance the kingdom of God on earth, it was not long before the church began to look upon itself as an end in itself and was able to identify its own security with the welfare of mankind. What wonder that it gradually took on an attitude of arrogance! Instead of soliciting support, it demanded it, daring

136

to penalize people for not attending its appointed services of worship, even presuming to persecute people who dared to disagree with its pronouncements. Yes, organized religion in all ages has been tempted to overlook why it was organized. Too often it has become the enemy of vital religion, the foe of progress, a bulwark of oppression, an instrument of reaction and inquisition, as it did during the middle ages, for example. It was then that the church forgot that the church was made for man and not man for the church. Instead of serving the needs of the people, it demanded that the people serve its needs. It became a law unto itself. But the inevitable reaction set in. The humanitarian protest of the Savonarolas and the Martin Luthers brought society back to its senses so far as western civilization was concerned. They called a halt to the exaltation of the church as an end in itself so that today the church is no longer quite the tyrant that it once was and would still tend to become if it were not for this challenge of the humanitarians—the vigilant liberals in all ages.

Is there danger of the church today making its organization an end in itself? There is such a danger. A great amount of time, energy and money is now being expended in most ecclesiastical circles from coast to coast on the mechanics of organization. I am sure that the prophetic figures of yesteryear would be somewhat shocked at the amount of time, energy, and money being expended today on the mechanics of organization. I think they would regard it as a peril to the purposes for which the church was called into being. We are not organized for the purpose of organization. There is a point to which every church should grow but in what respect? Every human body should grow, but there is a point beyond which growth endangers the life of the individual, and there is a point, an optimum point, beyond which it is not healthy for a church to grow. To become bogged down in organization, and forget the original purpose for which the church was organized is one of the great perils confronting religion today as in the past. There are many ministers who share this concern. The true liberal has no desire to abolish the church or to abolish organization. He recognizes that the instrument

137

must be as efficient as possible. He would preserve the church and use it but only as a means to serve the spiritual advancement of the human soul—never as an end in itself.

By the same token, the liberal proclaims the priority of man over the institution of marriage. Designed in the beginning to protect the interests of children, to simplify family relationships, to sanctify the affections of men and women, there are those who would make a sacrament of marriage, who look upon it as an end in itself, and insist that the union of two people must be preserved in every instance, regardless of the welfare of the individuals it was ordained to advance. Now to take the position that all marriages are made in heaven and should therefore not be dissolved under any circumstances is to ignore the realities of life. For there are clearly some marriages which were not made in heaven, which complicate domestic relations, which do not bring heaven on earth but hell on earth, and especially for the children who may be involved. Now the true liberal would not abolish marriage or make light of it, but he would recognize that it has its abuses as well as its uses and that some marriages were better dissolved than kept intact. Therefore, the true liberal believes in divorce, but he would be reluctant to use divorce except as a last resort, as a surgical operation involving risks. You know sometimes we have to cut out something that is cancerous in the human body, and so it is in family life. There are some people who should never marry at all; there are others who should never have married the mates they did. So when the sacramentalist insists, "What God hath joined together, let no man put asunder," the liberal replies, "Yes, but what God has put asunder, let no man join together, and if joined together, it is unwise to keep them so joined without the sanctity of love."

Now what about the institutions of free enterprise and labor unions?

Let us discuss these two together because they are intimately related. I wonder how many of us realize what a multitude of laws are behind these two institutions. It is quite natural for us here in this country to take both for granted as though they had always existed. Few of us fully realize

138

that both are creations of human society to serve the general welfare.

There are many countries today where the system of free enterprise and the system of labor unions do not exist. To establish the fact that they are both institutions, it is only necessary to imagine what would have happened to either one of them had Nazi Germany won the second world war and had overrun this country. Is there any doubt about it? Free enterprise as we have known it would have been destroyed. Labor unions would have been ordered to disband as they were in Germany under Hitler. There certainly would not be any labor strikes going on in our country today if the Nazis had won, and there would not be any choice for management but to accept compulsory arbitration. There is no doubt in my mind that if Communism were to prevail over the world, the same thing would be true.

Now the point I am trying to make is that both free enterprise and the labor union were established in this country to serve our way of life by serving the general welfare, and that neither one is sacrosanct in itself, and that what has been established can and will be dis-established or greatly modified if it does not fulfill the purposes for which it was organized. Now free enterprise was originally designed as the most likely economic system to insure general prosperity and the employment of all capable of employment by letting the law of supply and demand govern entirely the rewards of both capital and labor. When free enterprise does not work, it is because it is no longer free enterprise; we have hamstrung it.

By the same token, labor unions were permitted to come into existence to protect the interests of those dependent upon others for employment to enable labor to engage in collective bargaining, to insure responsible workmanship, to prevent labor from becoming a mere commodity, and thus to promote the general welfare ultimately.

In both institutions, however, abuses have crept in. Some free enterprises have sought and in many instances have secured what amounts to monopoly privileges. Thus being able to destroy legitimate competition, upsetting the law of supply and demand, and because of the power they can wield these have endangered the system of free enterprise itself. And in the same manner labor unions have employed tactics and fostered programs that are hostile to the general welfare. Not all of them but too many have sanctioned unnecessary and therefore, uneconomic duplications of effort in order to insure more jobs for their particular crafts. In some instances, they have practiced racial discrimination in certain parts of the country and raised up artificial barriers for membership. Obtaining the right to peaceful picketing, they have resorted to violence in many instances. They too have allowed the possession of power to endanger the system of the labor union, whenever they have used their hard won right to strike without regard to the general welfare, overlooking the fact that all rights involve corresponding responsibilities, and that continued irresponsible use of any right will eventually create a demand for its curtailment or even its complete abolition.

Now the true liberal attitude toward free enterprise and toward labor unions is that neither institution is an end in itself or beyond the power of people to alter by law, and that both must learn to subordinate their interests voluntarily to the interests of the country as a whole or eventually be compelled to submit to even more drastic legislation than is now being contemplated.

What is the liberal attitude toward the institution of government? Thank heaven we are able to raise such a question openly in this country without fear of being put into jail as citizens are in some countries. Only a few years ago we fought a successful war against an arrogant state that presumed to be a law unto itself. We won a military victory over Nazi Germany. Herr Hitler who deified government has been destroyed, but has Hitlerism been destroyed? Has the Nazi concept of the state been dethroned? On the contrary, it seems to me, to be still a formidable menace to reckon with. The exaltation of most institutions of society as ends in themselves has been successfully challenged in most countries throughout the world and is meeting with more or less conscientious resistance. But the exaltation of government still goes on, it goes on not only in Soviet Russia, but also in Franco Spain and in DeGaullist France. Yes, it is going on even in our own liberal country, under our own eyes, and in part with our help.

The centralization of power in the federal government, made necessary by the present struggle between the East and West, has greatly accelerated this insidious process of glorifying the state, as though our rights came from the state. Therefore we have allowed the rights of individuals which were once thought to be inviolate to be trampled under foot.

The government has pushed many people around unnecessarily. It has entangled us in a considerable amount of bureaucratic red tape. It has come to look upon itself as the source whence our rights and our blessings come. It is the temptation of all governments to become arrogant and dictatorial, to usurp power wherever and whenever they can. We have heard much warning about the threat of "the welfare state" to the liberties of our people but not enough warning about the far greater peril of "the warfare state." Here we are allocating more funds for armament than any nation in history, and it is the centralized power represented by these funds that constitutes the major hazard to our way of life even though its professed purpose is to defend our way of life. We have a growing bureaucratic octopus in this country. The time may come when we would like to get away from its tentacles. In his Farewell Address to the nation, Dwight D. Eisenhower warned us about "the acquisition of unwarranted influence, whether sought or unsought, by the military-industrial complex," and then went on to say "The potential for the disastrous rise of misplaced power exists and will persist." [71] This tendency toward centralization, it seems to me, must be courageously and intelligently kept under control. What happened to Rome, what happened to Greece, what happened to many other nations? It was this tendency for government to get so big that it becomes unwieldy. This must be resisted, because it is a tendency away from the original concept on which our republic was founded, which was essentially the liberal concept of government.

We read in the Declaration of Independence these words,

141

"We hold these truths to be self-evident, that all men are created equal; that they are endowed by their creator with certain unalienable rights; that among these are life, liberty, and the pursuit of happiness. That to secure these rights governments are instituted among men deriving their just powers from the consent of the governed; that whenever any form of government becomes destructive of these ends, it is the right of the people to alter or to abolish it and to institute new government." Here is precisely the point the liberal would emphasize. Government is an institution designed to serve the people. It is an instrument and nothing more. It has no inalienable rights of its own, not even the right of eminent domain, but whatever just powers it possesses are derived from the consent of the governed. The general trend of our age is away from this concept, not only in this country but in many other countries. The controls of government are being removed to centers more and more remote from the people. If we do no know our history in this respect, then we are bound to repeat the blunders of the past.

Against the arrogant state in all its forms the liberal must take his stand if he would remain true to the vision which has historically been his guide. He must proclaim the essential teaching of ethical religion, namely, "the infinite worth of every individual," and defend its modern implications, to insist not only that the Sabbath was made for man and not man for the Sabbath, but that church and state, marriage, private property, labor unions and all other institutions, were made for man and not man for these institutions; that nothing in this world is sacred except people and purposes and ideas, not things, not institutions, not organizations.

> We are all blind until we see
>   That in the human plan
> Nothing is worth the making if
>   It does not make the man.
>
> Why build these cities glorious
>   If man unbuilded goes?
> In vain we build the work unless
>   The builder also grows.[72]

142

Clearly our work as liberals is cut out for us. The world today is only vaguely interested on how we stand on such questions as "the infallibility of the Bible," "the atonement of Jesus," "the virgin birth," "the bodily resurrection," but what it is going to be increasingly interested in is how we stand in this great struggle for human rights, how do we stand on the issues that vitally affect the general welfare. And if I do not miss my guess, our witness is going to be needed more in the future than ever in the past. A liberal theology looks well only when it walks arm in arm with a liberal sociology. Yes, we have to go down the line for the dignity of man on all fronts. This should be our overall loyalty, our supreme goal.

Let us keep splendid loyalties,
For we are falling prey to lesser things.
What use are breath and strength if we no longer feel
The thrill of battle for some holy cause
Or hear high morning bugles calling us away?
Let brave hearts dare to break the truce with things
Ere we have lost our ancient heritage.
Are we to gain a world to lose our souls,
Souls which can keep faith until death
And die, triumphant, in some crimson dawn?
Nay, we must keep faith with the unnumbered brave
Who pushed aside horizons, that we might reach
The better things: We cannot rest until
We have put courage once more on her throne;
For honor clamors for her heritage,
And Right still claims a Kingdom of its own.[73]

Chapter 18

THE CHURCH MUST WIELD THE SWORD OF THE SPIRIT

Probably most people in this or any other generation prefer a religion that makes for unity and harmony, that emphasizes the agreements which men hold in common, rather than the differences which tend to keep them apart. The general tendency of our age is undoubtedly in the direction of ever closer cooperation among the various religious faiths, the healing of sectarian dissensions, and the harmonizing of divergent points of view. For example, the United Church in our neighboring country of Canada is a vital movement today. In this country several of our religious denominations have already merged or are about to do so. Good will meetings of Catholics, Protestants and Jews have been held in many parts of our country under the sponsorship of distinguished Rabbis, Priests and Ministers. And the World Council of Churches, which has gathered a large portion of Christendom into its organization, is now a going concern. This in my judgment is all to the good. Yes, "behold how good and pleasant it is for brethren to dwell together in unity!" [74] Surely one of the functions of a vital religion has ever been to bring the people of the world closer together and unite them in firm bonds of fellowship, understanding and cooperation.

And yet incredible and inconsistent as it may seem at first thought, another equally vital function of religion is to perform the very opposite task, namely, to call men out from the world, to persuade them to separate themselves from their fellow man, to organize them into militant minorities in order to challenge the complacency and inertia of the rest of mankind. In stressing the unifying and harmonizing function of religion we ought not to overlook its divisive role, for vital religion not only heals differences, it also tends to create differences. It would heal the differences that ought no longer to exist. It would create the differences that ought to be brought into existence.

"Think not," said Jesus, "that I am come to send peace on earth: I came not to send peace but a sword. For I am come to set a man at variance against his father, and the daughter against her mother, and the daughter in law against her mother in law, and a man's foes shall be those of his own household." [75] Here we have a declaration of spiritual purpose, which challenges the popular concept of what constitutes the mission of religion in this world. Surely it is difficult for us to think of Jesus, the lowly Nazarene, with a sword in his hand, is it not? We instinctively recoil from such a picture. For there are other things that look more appropriate in his hand than a sword and more consistent with the kind of life he actually lived. Here is Jesus! Put into his hand a shepherd's crook, and we say that is authentic, the good shepherd. Put into his hand a carpenter's awl and we recognize the horny-handed son of toil. Put into his hand a cruse of oil for the healing of wounds, or a martyr's cross, an Easter lily, or even a festal cup of wine, and the religious imagination accepts the picture as authentic, but place in his hands a sword and the same imagination recoils in horror. And yet if we can credit the gospel account Jesus emphatically declared, "Think not that I am come to send peace on the earth, I came not to send peace but a sword."

What could he have possibly have had in mind? What kind of a sword was it that he was preaching about? Could it have been the sword of violence, the symbol of strife and bloodshed, the weapon of those who would force their will upon the world? Did Jesus mean to countenance armed conflict as a method of establishing the kingdom of heaven on earth? Some of his fanatical followers of various kinds down through the centuries have tried to make out that he, whom we have agreed to call the Prince of Peace, explicitly sanctioned the use of arms and armament. But they have not succeeded in making a militarist out of Jesus. The task is

145

utterly hopeless. The record that we have of him, taken as a whole, indicates beyond any peradventure of a doubt that both his method and his spirit are far removed from those of force and violence. For he himself never attempted to resist his enemies by physical means. He deliberately chose to overcome evil with good. When he was in the Garden of Gethsemane and Peter assayed to protect him from arrest with his sword, Jesus rebuked that disciple bidding him to put away his sword saying, "They that take the sword shall perish by the sword." [76] Early in his ministry, when certain soldiers came to him for advice, he told them, "Do violence to no man." [77] The nearest that Jesus ever came to repudiating his own teaching in this respect was when he took the whip of cords and drove the money-changers from the temple. But even here there is no record that anyone was physically hurt; surely no blood was spilled, no life taken. With this one possible exception the character of his life and work was entirely opposed to the employment of physical force.

No, the sword that Jesus came to send on this earth, in my judgment, was not the sword of violence but the sword of the spirit, the sword of moral cleavage, the sword of prophetic challenge summoning men to separate themselves from their loved ones if necessary in order to engage in Messianic enterprise. "I am come to set a man against his father and the daughter against her mother and the daughter in law against her mother in law and a man's foes shall be those of his own household." Ethical religion, prophetic, vital religion, always does this very thing. It divides people over moral issues. It sets them into conflicting spiritual camps. It is a disrupting force, a severing power, a sundering factor in human society. It would detach men from their old associations, and former allegiances, and complacent ways, and send them forth to wage moral warfare, to wield the sword of the spirit against injustice, tyranny and immemorial wrongs, to do battle against the powers of darkness throughout the world, yes, even to disturb the peace of the world if that peace be the product of moral and spiritual inertia.

Vital religion is a unifying force, to be sure; that is what the word religion means, namely, "to bind together." But it is

146

also, when vital, a divisive force. Whenever it finds a people trying to worship both God and Mammon at the same time, prophetic religion says "ye cannot serve two masters, choose ye whom you shall serve." The sword of Hebrew prophecy cut off a small portion of the Hebrew people to become a saving remnant. The sword of Jesus brought division to many a home in Palestine. It brought division, at least a temporary division, into his own home. It set up a moral cleavage throughout the Roman empire. Later on the swords of John Huss and Martin Luther split the Christian world in twain. And in this country the swords of Wendell Phillips and William Lloyd Garrison disturbed the peace and harmony of our country for a whole generation. And in more recent times the swords of Walter Rauschenbush and Harry Emerson Fosdick have caused a cleavage in many a church throughout this land between those on the one hand who preach merely a gospel of personal piety and individual salvation and those, on the other, who preach also a gospel of civic righteousness and social salvation.

Vital religion summons us in this generation to take up once more the sword of the spirit. For grave social problems confront our country crying for solution. Great moral issues are before us demanding clarification. Within the immediate future we are going to be compelled by the onward march of events to take our stand on many important issues. For example, the question of the separation of church and state is bound to come up again and again as a challenge we cannot escape or ignore. What constitutes justice in the relations of capital and labor is also going to come up. It has already come up in California and Ohio, and it is going to come up in other states in the near future, in the form of proposed "right to work laws" and legislation concerning strikes against the public interest. How shall we stand on these issues? How far shall we go in centralizing the control of our economic life in the Federal government or can it be safely entrusted in the hands of free enterprise? We are going to be compelled whether we like it or not to take a stand.

And what about our relations with Soviet Russia, Red China and the whole communist world? Can the West and the East reach some agreement to get along together in the same world in spite of their obvious differences? Or shall both go on risking mutual destruction in atomic war? Above all, what about the problem of achieving first class citizenship for our colored fellow Americans? Now why do I say above all? Because I believe the differences between the United States and Soviet Russia may be solved before we solve this problem of race. The United States and Russia, whether under the Czars or the Soviets, have never gone to war with each other. There is no legacy of bitterness and hatred to be overcome in order for us to reach some kind of an agreement. The North and the South of this country fought a terrible war over the question of race, and we are still fighting it. I believe that this is the problem that is going to be most stubborn of solution. We must find a solution of which both the North and the South can be proud before the world and not ashamed. Racial discrimination in my judgment is the Achilles' Heel of our democracy, the weakest link in our chain of national defense. This problem must be solved in this generation. We have no time to lose. Either we abolish second class citizenship within the foreseeable future or run the grave risk of bringing down upon our heads the moral condemnation of three-fourths of mankind and thereby losing our opportunity for moral leadership in the world.

Yes, these are some of the major questions on which there is likely to be more and not less controversy in the years that lie immediately ahead. American citizens everywhere are going to be challenged to make moral choices even more than in the recent past. And the church along with others is going to be profoundly involved, whether we like it or not. It is going to mean controversy. Shall we be afraid of controversy? Let us not forget that the liberal faith was born in controversy, has thrived on controversy and will continue to justify its existence in the future only so long as it has the fortitude to engage in controversy whenever morally necessary. The mandate of our heritage requires us to risk being at variance with our brethren, in order to perform the prophetic role of religion and yet at the same time to recognize its unifying role as well that bids us to make every effort to hold all people together in the bonds of fellowship and good will. Let the church in the future as in the past fear not to take up the sword of the spirit wherever and whenever moral issues are at stake, but to do so, after the example of Him, who would have us love one another even as he loved us. In short, we must make bold to create the differences that ought to be and at the same time endeavor to heal the differences that ought no longer to exist.

CHAPTER 19

IMMORTALITY IS STILL A RATIONAL HOPE

If a man die, shall he live again? [78] This query posed long before the day of Job is one of the most baffling and yet fascinating questions of this or any age. "What about immortality? Is it still a rational hope?"

I know that to some this chapter will seem an utter waste of time and words. You have made up your minds on this issue, and have come to the conclusion that there is no convincing reason for you to believe in any life beyond the grave. Therefore, why discuss the question, when no one really knows the answer? The possibility of immortality seems so fantastically remote to you that for all practical purposes you have dismissed the concept from your scheme of things, and have long since adjusted your lives to what you believe to be the realities of existence. To all such, let me say that I feel like bowing before you in reverential envy. Anyone who can live this life here in the fullness of joy, and in enthusiastic, unselfish service of his fellow man, without being troubled by the obvious brevity of its span, surely deserves our highest respect and admiration. Undoubtedly there are many who succeed in doing so.

There are others, of course, who are not interested in this question at all, one way or the other, because they claim to possess no appetite for immortality. One life is enough for them. The thought of endless oblivion is a comforting rather than a disturbing thought. They have either lived so abundantly that they are completely satisfied with one life or they have lived so miserably that they do not want to contemplate the risk of its repetition. There is nothing they would like to do so much as to go to sleep and sleep forever.

There are many people, however, who have an entirely

different attitude toward this question. Most people have a very real interest in it, and I think I am safe in saying that the vast majority of the people I meet have a keen and wistful desire to keep on living indefinitely. Oh, they might welcome a refreshing nap for awhile, in order to rest from the anxieties of life, but not too long a nap. They love life far too much to spend any more of it than necessary in recuperative sleep. Therefore, the thought of sometime never being able to wake up is repugnant to their imaginations.

So keen and wistful is this desire to live on, that many people take considerable comfort in the thought that, come what may, they will continue to live on, at least in their children and their children's children, while something of the work they have wrought during their span of life may remain after they are dead and gone to influence future generations even though their names may be entirely forgotten. Vital, satisfying and inspiring as the hope of survival by way of one's descendants or the work of one's hands truly is, there are those who cherish the hope of a more personal survival. They want to live on themselves. They want their own self-consciousness to persist. They desire to keep on preserving their own individuality.

Now it has been argued that this desire to live on after death is a very selfish desire, but I, for one, have never been impressed with such an argument. I cannot see how it is any more selfish to want to live beyond this life than it is to want to live beyond this day. Surely most of us desire to live on at least until tomorrow morning, do we not? There is a valid distinction between selfishness on the one hand and self-interest on the other. Selfishness is the pursuit of our own self-interests at the expense of the self-interests of others. If the desire for personal survival after death were necessarily to call for the sacrifice of the self-interests of others, it would indeed be selfish, but of course it does not. It is therefore, morally, a legitimate desire. The question remains, is it also a rational desire? In short, what ground have we for cherishing the hope that such a desire has any real promise of being fulfilled?

Long before Jesus was born, there were scholarly and

151

intelligent men in India, in Palestine, in Greece, in Rome, in Egypt, and may other countries who held that the survival of human personality after death, while not established, is a reasonable hope. For example, there were Hillel and Philo among the Jews, Socrates and Plato among the Greeks, Cato and Cicero among the Romans. And after Jesus, there were Seneca and Epictetus, Roger Bacon and Francis Bacon (both associated with formulating the theory of the scientific method). Then there were Maimonides, Abelard, and a host of others. All these were intellectually convinced that immortality is a reasonable hope.

Listen to what Cicero had to say on this question and remember that Cicero was born about a century before the beginnings of the Christian era. He said:

> When I consider the faculties with which the human soul is endowed, its amazing celerity, its wonderful power of recollecting past events and its sagacity in discerning the future, together with its numberless discoveries in the arts and sciences,—I feel a conscious conviction that this active, comprehensive principle cannot possibly be of a mortal nature. And as this unceasing activity of the soul derives its energy from its own intrinsic and essential powers, without receiving it from any foreign or external impulse, it necessarily follows that its activity must continue forever. . . . I consider this world as a place which nature never intended for my permanent abode; and I look on my departure from it not as being driven from my habitation but simply as leaving an inn.[79]

Has anything been discovered since the days of Cicero that makes such a faith any less reasonable than it seemed to him? Has modern higher criticism, modern psychology, modern philosophy, or modern astronomy placed any insuperable difficulties in the way of such a hope? Have they jointly, or separately, uncovered any new evidence or brought forth any new arguments of fundamental significance that were not already considered by the ancients? It seems to me that a review of the facts will disclose that the hope of immortality, if it ever were a rational hope, is just as rational today as it ever was.

Let us consider some of the questions raised first by the higher critics, then by the modern psychologists, modern materialists, and then by the astronomers.

In the first place, what about the challenge of the higher critics? Have these scholars not demonstrated the improbability of Christ's physical resurrection from the tomb on Easter morn by proving, first, the contradictory character of the Gospel evidence and then, also, how unsupported it is? As a consequence has there not been a widespread loss of faith in immortality among modern men? This, of course, is undoubtedly true, but what of it? Is it not also true that the philosopher's arguments for the immortal hope does not rest upon such a basis as Christ's alleged bodily resurrection from the tomb on Easter morning? Long ago Voltaire, Descartes, Thomas Paine, Immanuel Kant, rejected the Easter legends of Christianity, and yet they firmly believed in the survival of life after death. And long before them, a whole line of Greek and Roman philosophers, who never heard about Jesus or the story of his resurrection, were yet able to find a rational foundation for their hope. We of the modern liberal faith who believe in the possibility of life to come do not rest our faith upon any physical resurrection or resuscitation alleged to have taken place some 1900 years ago. We can see no encouragement for the rest of mankind in the mere revival of life in one human body, even if it did take place, as it has taken place in our own day with the application of adrenalin to a heart that has ceased to beat. Resuscitation is not resurrection. Revival of life is not survival of life. We who believe we have a rational hope do not rest that hope upon the nature of the human body, but upon the intrinsic characteristics of the human soul. Therefore, we are not at all disturbed by the collapse of the Christian dogma of the bodily resurrection. Apparently the Apostle Paul did not rest his faith upon any physical resurrection, for it was he who said, "Flesh and blood cannot inherit the kingdom of God." [80]

In the second place, what about the challenge of modern

psychology? The more popular sophistication today is telling us that man is the victim of his own illusions, ever trying to run away from the harsh realities of life to take refuge in an imaginary world of his own creation. All who believe in the theory of the escape mechanism would have us believe that the hope of immortality is just a means of escape, that Easter is merely the dramatization of human gullibility—weak, wistful, gullible man building a paradise in the sky to avoid the necessity of finding, here and now, a happy issue to the only life that he will ever know. "How can desire be the basis of any reasonable hope," they argue. "Man wishes for many things here, but that does not make his wishes come true." Well, the ancients considered this problem too. They of course had never heard of Freud or Adler or Jung, but they were all acquainted with the phenomena of escape, even though they probably never used that word. For in the book of Job, the book of Wisdom, Psalms and the writings of the Greeks, Romans and Hindus, you will find warning after warning against the deceitfulness of the human heart. A man is often led astray by the mirages of his imagination. But those ancients also came to the conclusion that when desire and imagination are raised to the level of faith, then things begin to happen in this world, because these are the creative factors which bring to pass what otherwise could not take place. It was Paul who said, "Faith is the substance of things hoped for." Schopenhauer, the philosopher, said, "Desire is the constructive power behind evolution." Einstein not long ago said, "Imagination is greater than knowledge." Desire, imagination, faith! These things are creative factors in this universe. And it has been suggested by Professor William MacDougall of Duke University that perhaps the desire for immortality and the imagination to believe in it, are the prerequisites of human survival. After all, this might be true. And if it were true, would not the postulate of extinction, which many hold today, be the escape mechanism of spiritually tired people, too exhausted to make the effort to meet the conditions of survival, if these be the conditions? And let us not overlook the fact that there are many ways of running away from the realities of life, and that apathy, indifference, and cynicism may be among them.

In the third place, what about modern materialism? There are thinkers who insist that matter and energy are the last word in this universe, that human consciousness is but the product of chemical and physical forces, the happy accident of a fortuitous collision of atoms and electrons. Well, what about it? Is there anything essentially new in these contentions? Anything fundamentally new? Were not the ancient Greeks familiar with the philosophy of materialism? Did not the ancient Hebrews feel the force of its argument? Listen to this sigh of pessimism which has been preserved for us in the book of Wisdom:

> Short and sorrowful is our life; and there is no healing when a man cometh to his end, neither was any man known to return from the grave. Because by mere chance were we born, and hereafter we shall be as though we had never been; for the breath in our nostrils is smoke, and our reason is a spark kindled by the beating of our heart, which being extinguished, the body shall be turned to ashes, and the spirit shall be dispersed as thin air; and our life shall pass away as the traces of a cloud.[81]

Who in modern times has expressed the philosophy of materialism in any clearer language? And yet the author of the book of Wisdom after duly considering this argument goes on to declare—

> Thus reasoned they, and they were led astray; for their own ignorance hath blinded them. For God created man to be immortal, and made him an image of his own eternity. In the eyes of the foolish they seem to die; and their departure is accounted to be misery, and their journeying from us to be their ruin; but they are in peace. For the souls of the righteous are in the hand of God, and there shall no evil touch them.[82]

Yes, if the ancients were able to confront the argument of materialism, and yet rise to the conviction that the soul of man is stamped with the image of eternity, is not the immortal hope just as reasonable today as it ever was?

But suppose the assumption of the materialists be true? And let us not overlook the fact that it is only an assumption, and one which many of the scientists today are rapidly discarding, for what we are dealing with now is pretty much the philosophy that has been handed down to us from the middle of the nineteenth century, not the science of most of the modern scientists today. But suppose that the materialist philosophy be true. Suppose, for example, that self-consciousness is but the mere product of chemical and physical forces. Given an infinite period of time, is it not reasonable to believe that this same accident, which we call ourselves, might happen again and yet again? Why could not the same combination of atoms and electrons, which make up our bodies and this universe at this very moment, come into existence an indefinite number of times in the course of countless eons? A billion or a trillion years of oblivion would then be but a single night, and birth and death would be but the morning and evening of an oft repeated day. Thus, even on the basis of materialism, the hope of immortality is at least theoretically possible. I confess, however, that I do not place any confidence in the argument. And why? I cannot believe that this thing that we call the center of our life is a mere product of chemical and physical forces.

Consider the heroic example of Winston Churchill defying the might of the German military machine, when that machine was raining down death and destruction on the city of London during those awful days of the Second World War. I find the argument of materialism, which I once accepted, now requires more credulity than I can possibly summon. Explain the influence and the power and the courage of Winston Churchill defying that might as the mere result of chemical and visible forces? The idea is not only inadequate, to my mind, it is obviously absurd. The physical power of Churchill was as a small grain of sand in the path of a mountain avalanche. By the laws of physics and chemistry that avalanche would have crushed that grain of sand, but the grain of sand resisted the mountain avalanche. No, we must look for some other explanation of the heroic example of Britain's grand old man than a physical explanation. It was a spiritual and moral power which he wielded, and we must look for the source of that power in a world of reality that as yet we have been unable to perceive or to measure. In the case of a man of Churchill's age, there is a center of awareness in him so constituted that it has already survived the coming and going of several bodies since his birth. He may well survive the decay of his present body.

What about the challenge of modern astronomy to the concept of life's survival? Have not our astronomers told us that they have scanned the firmament of the heavens and found no abode of the blessed? Have they not also shown that this is a limited universe? How can this universe, big as it is, be big enough to contain all the human souls and living beings which are perpetually coming into existence? Can there be such a thing as survival after death and such a place as the abode of the blessed? Surely by this time it would be overcrowded with the endless procession of pilgrims who have gone before. In other words, how can a limited creation possibly find room for all the personalities which have been brought into being down through the millenniums? If this thought has not occurred to you, at least it has challenged the attention of Professor William James of Harvard.

The ancient Hindus, Greeks, and Romans wrestled with this same problem, and they arrived at a rational solution. We must not overlook the fact that their universe was a much more limited one than ours, yet they found room for all the spirits believed to depart hence. The Hindus gave a rational answer by denying that the soul of man is created at birth, postulating its pre-existence and its indestructibleness, claiming it to be an eternal entity which ever takes unto itself new and fresher forms of physical expression. The number of souls being limited, there is thus no danger of crowding a limited universe. Some of the Greeks and Romans gave a rational answer to this question by denying that the soul of man occupies any space whatsoever. They postulated the theory that spirit is something different from matter and therefore not subject to quantitative measurement, possessing

157

neither dimension nor weight. Therefore the problem of a crowded universe was no more a problem to them, but as ridiculous as the anxiety of the medieval scholastics over the number of angels who could dance on the point of a pin seems to us now. Please do not jump to any conclusions.

I am neither upholding the Greek doctrine of an immaterial soul, nor the Hindu doctrine of a pre-existent one, although both theories have merit and both may be true. I am only contending that modern astronomy with its revelation of a limited universe has not added anything new to the problem of faith, and that, if the hope of immortality were ever a rational hope, it is fully as rational today as in the days of Socrates and Cicero.

There are many who hold that there are more substantial grounds for the hope today than at any other time in human history. For we possess the findings of the British and American Societies for Psychical Research, which were not available to the ancients. Science today offers no adequate denial of the possibility of immortality and submits facts that may reasonably be interpreted as suggestive of its reality. I am wondering how many professors and scientists, as well as average laymen, have made anything more than a cursory examination of the great mass of evidence which the British and American Societies for Psychical Research have uncovered and brought together—a mass of evidence which when impartially considered, as it so seldom is, confronts us with something of the dilemma that either something of human personality does survive the death of the physical body or that the subconscious mind of man operates in such a far-ranging manner, independent of time and space, as to give rise to the conclusion that it must belong in an altogether different category of being than that of the physical form.

I happen to belong to a group of liberal clergymen including humanists and theists alike, who for some time now have been making a serious study of the findings of the British and American Societies for Psychical Research. This science is also known as Parapsychology and Extrasensory perception. I have discovered that the reports of these two societies have had a much wider acceptance among the scientists in Great Britain, for example, than they have in this country. But even here, there are professors at Harvard, Stanford, Duke, Clark, and several other respectable universities who are making careful experiments in this once disreputable field, under the protection of generous endowments for this specific purpose. And yet this new science is still in its groping stage. In my judgment it has already uncovered enough facts to show that the question of immortality is still an open question, and the hope for it is still a rational one.

I am convinced that what we call human personality is something more than the result of the chemistry of a slowly dying fire. I am convinced that there is a center of awareness in man that survives the coming and going of many bodies, and that this center is an intrinsic part of this universe, as intrinsic as the electron and the dust of constellations. I am convinced that we are only in the early dawn of understanding what its true nature is, or what its final destiny is like. But as some of us grope and make our way in the early dawn, we believe that we discern the image of immortality stamped upon it, an image which will be more clearly revealed when the full noontime of scientific knowledge has come.

Every advance in scientific knowledge made thus far has disclosed not a less wondrous universe but a more wondrous universe than man in his wildest dreams imagined before such advances had been made. And we may well believe that, when the scientific method has been adequately applied to the study of the human personality, the facts uncovered, the truth disclosed, will astound man's imagination, expand his whole horizon, and exalt his sense of dignity and worth as never before, since he first began to ponder the meaning of life and his own destiny.

CHAPTER 20

PARAPSYCHOLOGY IS WORTHY OF SERIOUS CONCERN

The findings of parapsychology are worthy of serious consideration. Parapsychology is merely a new word for what used to be called psychical research. It is the study of telepathy, clairvoyance, clairaudience, precognition, psychokinesis and the other forms of extra-sensory perception. I take it that the word parapsychology has been introduced to supplement the connotations of psychical research, because the latter has been associated in the popular mind with the study of *abnormal* behavior—such as mediumship, trances of the seance room, and so forth, whereas the emphasis of the parapsychologist today is on the more normal behavior of men and women, although it does not exclude any of these other phenomena.

This chapter is based in part on a book published by Dr. J. B. Rhine of Duke University, entitled *The New World of the Mind,* which appeared a few years ago. I found it to be a most provocative and stimulating volume. It goes without saying that its subject matter has stirred up considerable controversy. But I venture to predict that if its methods and conclusions are sooner or later sustained by scientific criticism and analysis, then eventually it and its companion volumes could be assigned a place beside Darwin's *Origin of Species* and *Descent of Man* as opening up a new world of exploration for the human mind. It might, in other words, be included in tomorrow's list of Great Books, which our children will be urged to study if they would be truly educated.

Now the main conclusion to which Dr. Rhine and his associates have come, after several years of experimentation in their laboratory at Duke University, is that there exists an extra-physical element in man that does not seem to be subject to any of the laws already known to govern the physical universe. He calls it the "Psi factor." It is a short word for psychic capacity. This, of course, is the fundamental postulate in all the major religions of mankind. Professor Rhine is not telling the religious world anything new, for religion has all along stubbornly insisted on the existence of something in man, an agency, if you please, which uses the physical body as an instrument and is not therefore necessarily involved in its dissolution. And religion has asked mankind to accept this largely as a matter of faith and revelation. Now what is new in Professor Rhine's contention is that he and his associates claim to offer scientific evidence of the existence of the non-physical element in man. If you are among those who already believe in this fundamental postulate of religion and have never doubted it for a moment, then of course this chapter is like offering you proof when you do not need any. On the other hand, if you are among those who hold the opposite conviction, namely, that the so-called soul or mind of man is nothing but the product of chemical and physical forces, and are perfectly sure that everything has been said on this subject that can be said, then of course this chapter could easily be a waste of time and effort for you. But if you are like some among us, having been brought up in an orthodox faith, then having lost that faith upon coming in contact with scientific knowledge, you still do not know quite what to believe, yet hold that the existence of the non-physical element in man is still an open question, then what Professor Rhine has to offer should be of considerable importance, at least worthy of your critical examination, even if in the end you find yourself unable to accept either his method or his conclusions.

Dr. Rhine claims that the new evidence shows that some people may become aware of events taking place miles away from them. This is called clairvoyance. Also, some people can become aware of events that have not yet taken place. This is called pre-cognition. And some people seem to be able to influence matter without physical contact, as in those dice-throwing tests which they carry on at Duke University. This

161

is called psychokinesis. Dr. Rhine claims that perfectly normal people in good mental health make far better scores in these tests than those who are mentally ill or otherwise abnormal. Over in London University a distinguished British scientist, Dr. S. G. Soal, in an independent test, confirms in his laboratory in England, the findings of the Rhine experiments, and there have been departments of parapsychology in Vienna, Germany and France, and in other sections of the United States who would say "Amen" to these conclusions.

Now, what do scientists in general think about the experiments and the findings? The statistical method by which they determine the law of probability has been called into question, but in 1937 the American Institute of Mathematical Statistics, under the leadership of Professor Huntington of Harvard University, after an examination of the methods used at the Rhine laboratory, publicly endorsed this aspect of the investigation and said that their statistical method cannot be questioned.[83] In 1952 Dr. Lucien Warner sent a questionnaire to one third of the fellows of the American Psychological Association. He received 360 replies.[84] Roughly speaking, one sixth of the psychologists were willing to accept the occurrence of what is called extra-sensory perception as either established or a likely possibility. Five-sixths, however, replied that they do not consider the evidence thus far produced as acceptable. But more than two-thirds of these acknowledged that they had not read any of the original reports, and nearly one third stated that they had made up their minds against the existence of extra-sensory perception wholly on a-priori grounds—that is, the method of deductive reasoning as distinguished from inductive reasoning, which is the first method to be used by the scientist. In 1948 Doctor Russell MacRobert, a psychiatrist in New York City, sent out a similar questionnaire to his fellow psychiatrists, and he received 723 replies, among which 31 per cent claimed familiarity with the experiments, 68 per cent considered that such researches should be sponsored by them, 23 per cent testified that they had personally observed the phenomena in their own practices and experience, and only 17 per cent were uncertain.[85]

Now this more favorable attitude on the part of the

psychiatrists, as distinguished from the less favorable attitude of the psychologists, Professor Rhine explains as follows: "Psychiatrists, faced with the urgency of having to find cures for their patients, have always been more venturesome than the psychologists." I do not know whether that is true or not. He says, "They have, in fact, in many instances been forced to become research psychologists themselves and find out from their own studies much of what they have needed to know about the psychological make-up of the people they were trying to serve." He continues, "Looking back down the history of psychology, one can see that most of its greatest achievements, especially those relating to the deeper structure of personality . . . came from such pioneers on the medical front of psychology. Evidently orthodoxy is not quite so rigid in the psychiatric branch as in the other branches of the human sciences." And then this final word: "In whatever field exploration is still active, the fellow explorer is least likely to encounter resistance to his own discoveries." [86]

Now, what of my own attitude toward the Rhine experiments? It is of course the attitude of a layman, but I have been studying this subject for quite a number of years. I find myself still on the fence, but leaning definitely in the direction of Professor Rhine's conclusions. I hold that the whole area with which the parapsychologists are dealing is a worthy, important and legitimate field of scientific inquiry. I was started off in this direction by Professor James H. Hyslop of Columbia University. Over forty-five years ago I heard him make a statement in the Ford Hall Forum of Boston that the American and British Societies for Psychical Research had more facts assembled to establish the hypothesis of extra-sensory perception than Darwin and Wallace had when they announced the theory of evolution, and I have been interested ever since in this subject.

The scientific method has made remarkable discoveries in the physical sciences of biology, chemistry, medicine and astronomy. And why? Because the scientific method calls for the facts of life. It takes special pains to examine all the facts and to overlook none of them, if possible, and surely not to discard a single fact just because it does not fit in with the investigators' preconceptions. I believe that this same method should be applied to what goes on in the less tangible but no less real world of the human mind and emotions. We read a few years ago in the public press about a woman who claimed to awaken at three o'clock in the morning from a nightmare in which she saw her son die in a flaming plane crash. The next day a reporter telephoned her home to tell her that her son was aboard a plane which had crashed and caught fire at Seattle, but that he had suffered only minor bruises. The woman claimed that she did not know that her son was on the way home. In these words she described the scene of her dream. "I saw a plane leave a big airfield. There were civilians around, but mostly there were soldiers. Then I saw the house right in the way of the plane as it dived and caught on fire. I waited outside the wreck, helplessly waiting while man after man climbed out of the wreckage. Then I saw my own boy. He was burning, his clothes were on fire. He fell down, he did not move. I thought he was dead." Now, what actually happened was that the boy had been able to put out the fire and survive the ordeal. Was that a mere coincidence? Have we all the facts here? Or was there some causal connection between that woman's dream and the event that took place? I would like to know, because I have had similar dreams myself.

In 1918 I was on a steamship sailing from France approaching the harbor of New York City. It was about two o'clock in the morning and I had a dream of my younger brother dying. It was so vivid that the dream awoke me and I immediately got up out of my berth and made a note of it in my notebook—the hour and the details of the dream. I had not heard from this younger brother for at least three months during the war. I did not know that he had moved to Concord, New Hampshire. I had no knowledge that he had been attacked by Spanish influenza. So, when I arrived in New York I called up an older brother who came over to see me through the customs, and I told him about my dream. "Oh-h," he said, "there's nothing to it. I just heard from him a week ago; nothing is wrong." But that very afternoon he received a telegram that the younger brother was dying from Spanish influenza, and later another telegram at four o'clock that he had died. Was that a mere coincidence, or was there some causal connection? I do not claim to know the answer, but I should like to know. For if it were a coincidence, I could cite at least a dozen remarkable coincidences which have taken place in my own life and that of my immediate family, and not all have been confined to dreams either. Some of them have taken place while awake.

There is the striking example of the distinguished Swedish scientist Emanuel Swedenborg, who while fully awake described to guests gathered in his house the course of a fire taking place in a distant city. He tells the course of this fire, how at certain streets (naming the streets) the fire is successfully stopped, and how much damage it has done over the whole of that city. Later on, Swedenborg verified his startling vision. At any rate, he claimed that it was verified in every detail. Verified by whom? By Swedenborg and his friends. Can we accept such testimony? There were no telephones in his day. It was the eighteenth century, no telephones, no telegraphs. How could he have described in detail the process of a fire in that far away place unless telepathy or clairvoyance be a *fact?* And if a fact, then we have a form of communication that is independent of all known laws governing the customary forms of physical communication. For the intensity of light waves, heat, sound, radio and x-rays decreases directly in proportion to the square of the distance between the source and the point of observation. But in telepathy, clairvoyance, precognition, the interposition of distance does not seem to make any difference, and this naturally leads to the conclusion that either there must exist in man something spiritual or if physical, then some form of physical reality that goes beyond what we know.

Now what I want to know is whether this is a fact or a mere speculation. It seems to me that scientists should eventually be able to tell us one way or the other, and come to some general agreement. Furthermore, they should be able to tell us a great deal more than we now know about other aspects of man's inner being. For example, is there such a thing as free will? Our courts, our laws, our schools, our churches, our social conventions are based on the supposition that all men are accountable for their behavior. If there is no such thing as free will, if man is but a product of his heredity and environment, then our retributive system of justice is based upon a monstrous superstition and we ought to know about it.

All the religions encourage the practice of prayer. What evidence is there that praying does any good? What sound and tested teaching is there to prepare a man for such a final fact as death? Are there certain kinds of prayer in which we may engage that are scientifically valid and others that are a pure waste of time? We ought to know. We ought to apply the scientific method to these problems. And what evidence is there, for example, of survival after death? Have all the heavens and happy hunting grounds and Valhallas proclaimed by the various religions, not a shred of evidence to support these claims? Or are there substantial facts which a critical mind can examine and come to the conclusion that the hope immortal is still a rational hope?

A few years ago a sensational book was published entitled *The Search for Bridey Murphy*, in which an amateur hypnotist claimed to have hypnotized a young woman and taken her back into at least two previous incarnations, giving several alleged details of it. What truth is there to this claim? Is there such a thing as retrocognition, whereby the past can take place before our eyes as though present? Is there such a thing as reincarnation? Socrates held that his theory of immortality was based upon what he believed to be evidence for preexistence. A large number of the scholars of India believe that there has been an evolution of the human mind as well as of the human body. They accept the idea of reincarnation as the only rational explanation of life. There have been many men of the western world who have so believed—Cicero, Plato, Julius Caesar, Victor Hugo, Whitman, Tennyson, Browning, Longfellow, Swinburne, Thomas Huxley, Spinoza and Schopenhauer. But the fact that they have believed in it does not make it true, of course. It merely means that we should examine that theory, that is all.

The Swami Akhilananda, of Boston, who is a lecturer on comparative religion at Harvard University and on the Board of Chaplains at the Massachusetts Institute of Technology, told me recently about a Bridey Murphy case in India, with which he was familiar. It is the story of a young girl in her early teens, who suddenly had a vision of preexistence in India in which she had died in childbirth. She was able to describe in such detail the community in which she had formerly lived that her friends and neighbors were able to identify the place and direct the woman to it. He said the girl was able to go to that place and identify herself to her aged husband, still living, and identify herself to his entire satisfaction. The Swami said there were numerous cases like that in India which the scholars of India had recognized. He then gently stressed the importance of keeping an open mind on this question. Science, he declared, cannot afford to dismiss any alleged experience of the human race as unworthy of investigation. He insisted that even an hallucination is a fact which calls for an adequate explanation. You see a rainbow; when you get to the place where you think it should be, there is nothing there. But the rainbow is a fact. It requires an explanation. And then he went on to say, "Surely, the numerous experiences which highly educated people as well as less educated people have in India, claiming to recall former incarnations, are just as worthy of scientific study as the orbits of moons and planets, or the constitution of molecules and atoms." Then he inquired: "What is so incredible about preexistence? We believe in the preexistence of the chemicals which compose the human body, do we not? Why not in the preexistence of the life that animates them?" Then he declared, "Blind scepticism is just as much a hindrance to the discovery of truth as blind credulity." [87] And there I had to agree.

Science can be infected with orthodoxy as well as religion. Professor Charles Richet of France declares, "The history of all sciences warns us that the simplest discoveries have been rejected *a priori* as being incompatible with science. Medical anesthesia was denied by Majendie. The action of microbes was contested for twenty years by all the scientists of all the academies. Galileo was imprisoned for saying that the earth revolves. Bouillard declared that the telephone was but ventriloquism. . . . A volume could be written on the absurd criticisms with which every great discovery has been received." [87a]

What delayed the acceptance of Darwin's theory of evolution in university circles, more even than the opposition of the Catholic church or the opposition of the orthodox Protestant church? It was the orthodoxy of a great scientist, Louis Agassiz, who was the most distinguished naturalist in America at that time. It was his orthodoxy and that of other scientists that delayed the acceptance of the doctrine of evolution in university circles. When Dr. Franz Mesmer of Germany first announced the discovery of hypnotism, the cries that went up from the scientists were loud and harsh. Fraud, fraud, hypnotism is all a fraud! Today the scientific world regards hypnotism as an established fact, being used every day by many of our physicians and psychologists. The scientific method is one thing, the scientist is quite another and being human he can make mistakes like the rest of us.

Now, in conclusion, I do not want any one to misunderstand my own position on this question at issue. I am not saying that there is already substantial scientific evidence for all the conclusions put forth by Professor Rhine, only that enough evidence has been uncovered to date to suggest the possibility that further evidence may yet be forthcoming to put this whole controversial issue beyond the peradventure of a doubt, one way or the other. I believe that it is a legitimate and most important endeavor. Its labor should be encouraged rather than dismissed out of hand. In the meantime we cannot wait for all this new evidence to come in before at least arriving at some tentative conclusions of our own. You and I must live in the present and the present calls for a working philosophy of life, the best that we can get. In other words, we must believe now whether we want to or not, and we must believe in accordance with our whole spiritual and intellectual needs, as it were. Now, as far as I am able to judge, from the best evidence that I can get, and using what judgment has been given me, I believe there is an organizing agency in man that uses the physical body as an instrument, and is therefore not necessarily involved in the dissolution of the human body. Furthermore, I believe that this organizing agency could not have been created at birth, but has always existed, and by that token I would surmise that it is likely to continue to exist indefinitely. I believe that this life within our own is a segment of the great creative power which is behind all existence, which we have agreed to call by the name of "God"—that this God can be found within ourselves and identified as such. If we truly search, we can truly find, for this God can be communed with directly through prayer and meditation. All men so commune; the only difference between them being that some are more consciously aware of this communion than others and more effective. A wondrous power has supervised our entrance into this earthly existence. I was not aware of coming here voluntarily. It seems to me that we can trust that same power to supervise our departure from this life. What else can we do? I find that my own faith has been clearly expressed by the poet Frederick L. Hosmer:

> I came not hither of my will
>   Or wisdom of my own:
> That higher Power upholds me still,
>   And still must bear me on.

> I knew not of this wondrous earth,
>   Nor dreamed what blessings lay
> Beyond the gates of human birth
>   To glad my future way.

> And what beyond this life may be
>   As little I divine,—
> What love may wait to welcome me,
>   What fellowships be mine.

I know not what beyond may lie,
    But look in humble faith,
Into a larger life to die
    And find new birth in death.

Upon his providence I lean,
    As lean in faith I must;
The lesson of my life has been
    A heart of grateful trust.[88]

CHAPTER 21

HONEST AGNOSTICISM IS A MARK OF REVERENCE

A few years ago in our capital city a distinguished professor at George Washington University was dismissed because he had publicly confessed to being an agnostic concerning the existence of God.

The minister of a prominent church in that city, Dr. A. Powell Davies, rose to the support of that professor and denounced his dismissal as undemocratic and blasphemous. Among other things he declared, "God, being godly, is in no need of defense. What kind of God could he be who needed security measures to protect him. It is apostasy—all of it—and in a very deep sense, blasphemy, for God lives in the open mind, in the power of its thought, the voice of its truth, the inner impulse of its honesty. He needs no protection—no shelter—no defense. Just give Him room." [88a]

With this declaration, I am in whole-hearted agreement. The word "agnostic" should not be regarded as an epithet of contempt, for many honorable and distinguished men and women have called themselves "agnostics."

The word simply means—"I do not know."

There are certainly large areas of human interest and inquiry where we must confess our ignorance and doubt, if we would be truly frank and honest.

The poet, Alfred Tennyson, has observed:

> There lives more faith in honest doubt
> Believe me, than in half the creeds. [89]

There are many spiritual values which the agnostic has to contribute. It is his very sincerity which compels him to confess, "I do not know." Indeed, agnosticism should constitute a large part of every honest man's religion. There are certain questions in life to which we do not know the answers as yet, and the honest and courageous thing to do is to acknowledge our ignorance.

Dark mysteries, like enveloping clouds, surround our life on this planet. Whence came we at birth? Whither do we go at death? Why are we here? What is the meaning of our striving and struggling? Has it any meaning at all? Is there some cosmic intelligence, some universal mind guiding and controlling the destiny of man and the world in which he lives? Where is the priest or preacher, or rabbi, or theologian, or philosopher, or scientist who actually knows the answers to these questions? There are speculations, assumptions, theories and hypotheses but as far as *my* experience has gone, I have found *no* one who really *knows*. There are those who by consulting their dreams and desires, their hopes and wishes and longings have persuaded themselves that they know, and presume to speak as though they did, when, as a matter of fact, they are as much in the dark as the simple savage of the primeval forest.

Not long ago I heard an apparently intelligent preacher describe in great detail the will and plan of God for this generation. He spoke as familiarly of the Almighty as though he had just come from a round-table conference with Him, and had the latest report on the status of His mind. To me such an attitude was not only disappointing but thoroughly revolting. It was lacking in the spirit of true reverence. The spirit of true reverence, in my judgment, calls for an honest confession of ignorance concerning the great mysteries of life, rather than an unwarranted profession of inside information.

This ultra-orthodox preacher is only one among many who speak glibly and voluminously about things that they know little about. They are the dogmatists who make high-sounding assertions about God and Immortality and the destiny of man upon little or no evidence at all. In the long run, they prove to be a hindrance rather than a help to the cause of religious progress. They are the kind who have kept the world in bondage to ancient superstitions and outworn theologies long after the time when these should have been discarded by mankind. They are the believing dogmatists.

On the other hand we have the disbelieving dogmatists who make just as sweeping denials on insufficient evidence as the former make unwarranted affirmations. How many times I have gone to so-called radical meetings and secular societies and heard speakers make unsupported assertions that there is no God; that there is no intelligence behind the universe; that there is no such thing as life beyond the grave; that life has no meaning, and that all the love and beauty in this world and all the capacities of the human mind are but the accident of fate, the achievement of happy chance.

In my opinion, such sweeping denials go far beyond the little that we know and are just as irresponsible and as unwarranted an attitude as that of the dogmatists who take the opposite point of view.

To me, the honest agnostic takes the most defensible position toward all these metaphysical questions. His is neither the attitude of affirmation or denial, but the attitude of earnest inquiry. His is the open mind and the disciplined tongue. His is the sincerity of the truth-seeker, who makes no pretensions to knowledge when he has none, and avoids exaggerations when he has but little. His is the attitude which seems to me to be the most reverential in spirit and which holds out to the world the most hope of true religious progress.

As one who has gradually come to appreciate the spiritual significance of this point of view, let me explain in a general way my own position on the great metaphysical questions of existence.

First of all, whence came we at birth? Are we the mere product of chemical and physical forces operating according to blind law? Or does the spark of life originate in some outside source? "Like trailing clouds of glory do we come from God, who is our home?" As a preacher with a theological training, I suppose I ought to have a definite answer to give, but as a matter of fact I have not. As a child I was taught to believe that I was specially created by an Almighty God in Heaven and that a kind and loving angel brought me to this earth. I was even shown the window through

173

which the angel came. I confess I would like to believe that my advent to this planet was part of a deliberate plan of an all-wise and beneficent Being. I think I would have more confidence in myself. I am inclined to believe, however, that our psychical as well as our physical equipment is the product of a long-drawn-out process of development and evolution. I am inclined to believe not only that the substance of our bodies but the substance of our minds has had a previous existence. That you and I are spiritually what we are today because of a multitude of past experiences, the bulk of which antedate our physical birth,—experiences which we have long since forgotten, so far as our conscious minds are concerned, but which we have stored away in the treasure-house of our inmost being.

I am inclined to believe, with Wordsworth—

> Our birth is but a sleep and a forgetting;
>   The soul that rises with us, our life's Star,
> Hath had elsewhere its setting
> And cometh from afar.[90]

It is a belief which has been cherished by millions, all the way from Socrates and Buddha to Herman Keyserling and Mahatma Gandhi. This is the tendency of my faith today. If you ask me what I know, I am compelled to answer "comparatively nothing." Whence came we at birth? I answer reverently, "I do not know. Do you?"

The second great metaphysical question is as difficult as the first—whither do we go at death? The body returns to the elements of which it is composed. It disintegrates into dust and ashes. This we know. There is no need of agnosticism on this point. But is there something else in man, less tangible, less ephemeral, which survives the shock of death? That is the great question of the ages. Again, as a minister of religion, as a conductor of funeral services, I suppose I ought to have a definite answer, but I confess that I have *not*. I comfort the sorrowful and the lonely if I am able to comfort them at all with the consolation of hope and faith, not with the consolation of facts and knowledge. I wish I knew. I once

174

thought I did. One of the earliest recollections of my child-hood is that of an Easter tableau in which some one personifying an angel blew a trumpet and I was surprised to see a number of apparently dead children suddenly come to life. Thus was the doctrine of the physical resurrection impressed upon me in my tender years. Later on I was taught to believe that while the bodies of the dead would never come to life again, the soul would obtain a new and different kind of body after death; that it would be even more useful and more beautiful than the old body; and that our friends on the other side of the grave would surely recognize us and we would surely recognize them and everyone would be a great deal happier.

This was what I was taught to believe and what I actually did believe for many years, and I confess that I would like to believe it now. I am wistful enough to wish it were true.

I am inclined, however, to put my faith in a different kind of immortality, but none the less vital.

I am inclined to hold that if there is any survival after death, it is confined to that part of us which we call our subconscious minds. Perhaps this is the only important and precious part of us anyway.

I am inclined to believe that this subconscious self is an intrinsic and eternal factor in this universe, uncreated and indestructible, beginning life on the other side of the grave exactly where it leaves off here, acquiring and assimilating new experiences with the potentiality of progressing forever onward and upward.

This is the general tendency of my faith today. If you press me for proof, if you call for the facts, I shall have to confess my utter lack of knowledge. I have long been seriously interested in the investigation of the phenomena of extra-sensory perception as conducted by the British and American Societies for Psychical Research. The findings of this investigation suggests the possibility that the human mind may be quite independent of the human brain and therefore that something of human personality may survive the disintegration of the physical body. But this is inference and not assurance.

Whither do we go at death? Again I reverently answer, "I do not know. Do you?"

The third great question which has perplexed the mind of man is the meaning of existence. What are we here for? Are we here for some great purpose, or no purpose at all? Even if the life of man is bounded by birth on the one side and death on the other, has this life anything more than earthly significance? Is there no cosmic life to which we minister? Again as a preacher of religion, I suppose I ought to speak with the conviction of certainty. The masses of the people are looking for such assurance, but I cannot in truth speak with certainty. What is the meaning of existence? What are we here for? The creeds and catechism, of course, have a ready answer. Man is here to praise God, and enjoy Him forever. The meaning of existence is to be found in serving the will of an all-wise, all-powerful and beneficent Deity, whose commands are the very laws of the universe, whose purpose is the great goal towards which the whole creation moves. That is what I was taught to believe in my youth and that is what I once devoutly cherished, and I am not ashamed to say that I would like to be able to hold the major portion of such a creed today.

I would like to believe, for instance, that there exists some supreme intelligence behind the phenomena of life—*not* the vindictive and arbitrary Deity of John Calvin and Jonathan Edwards, nor the sensual divinity of the Greeks and Romans, but some one like the heavenly Father of Hosea and Jesus who watches over us as earthly parents guard their children. I confess that since considerable doubt has been cast upon this idea in my own mind, this universe for me is a much less cozy place in which to live than it was before. The spiritual atmosphere may be more bracing and invigorating but it is also decidedly more chilly. I am still moved to believe, however, that there is some cosmic parent of us all, some intelligence at the foundation of existence, some creative power at the heart of things, limited no doubt by chemical and physical forces, limited in knowledge and experience, an evolving Deity of whom we are a spiritual part, in whom we live and move and have our being, with whom we labor as co-creators of the world that is to be, and about whom we can only know as we plumb the depths and scale the heights of our own minds and spirits. The ultimate reality is surely something more than mechanistic,—it is at least organic, and probably sentient and purposive. This is the direction of my faith today. If you press me for what I *know* and insist on scrutinizing the sources of my information then I am compelled to throw up my hands in almost utter helplessness. I have no body of data which would pass as scientific evidence.

Drive me into an intellectual corner on any *one* of these three great questions which we have been discussing and I shall have to acknowledge my own agnosticism. I simply do not know the answer, and I know of no one else who does,—and what I do not know I refuse to preach and teach as if I did, for in this direction lies intellectual dishonesty and spiritual degradation.

*   *   *

There are some things, however, that I *do know* which are fraught with tremendous significance and about which none of us needs to be agnostic.

I know from the experiences of others and some I have had myself that those people who are the happiest are engaged in some form of creative labor—men who bring things to pass that never before existed—women who give birth to children or mold their minds and characters—youths who strive to make their dreams come true; that there are none so miserable as they who have so little to do that they find time hanging heavily on their hands.

I know from the experiences of others, and some I have had myself that the committal of one's loyalties and energies to some great cause outside of one's self eventuates in a joy and satisfaction that can come in no other way.

I know from the experiences of others and some I have had myself that words of forgiveness and acts of generosity bring spiritual blessings to ourselves as well as others.

I know that self-respect, the good will of friends and the domestic affections are among the richest possessions that any one can strive for and acquire.

I know that the blood which flows in the veins of all

177

races is of the same color, that black and white and brown and yellow are brothers and sisters of one another, progeny of some common parentage who owe to one another the sustained consideration becoming to members of one family.

I know that warfare and peonage and economic exploitation, retributive punishment, religious intolerance and all forms of hatred are incompatible with this relationship.

I know that there is an infinite life within our own constantly prompting us to reach out for that which is beyond our immediate grasp, to give ourselves to those things in life which shall outlast life itself and that only as we trust and obey these promptings do we feel that we are not living in vain.

I know that if the spirit of brotherhood is some day to prevail over this earth you and I must follow more closely in the footsteps of the world's Christs and begin here and now to put more of their spirit into our own lives and do all we can to discourage those agencies and factors that tend to foster an opposite spirit.

Man's love for man, dim lantern that it still is, is after all the brightest light we have wherewith to beat back the darkness of the cosmic mystery that surrounds our planetary existence.

Agnostics in theology? Yes. Agnostics on moral, social and spiritual matters. Far from it. The facts of life in these respects are plentiful enough to call for clean-cut affirmations.

Therefore without intellectual misgivings or moral reservations we may yet preach and teach the gospel of a dynamic and inspiring religion.

Rabindranath Tagore, India's great seer and poet, discloses the basic fact upon which all dynamic religion rests when he declares:

Within us we have a hope that always walks in front of our present narrow experience; it is the undying faith of the infinite in us; it will never accept any of our disabilities as a permanent fact; it sets no limits to its own scope; it dares to assert that man has oneness with God and its wild dream comes true everyday.[91]

CHAPTER 22

WE MUST UNDERSTAND THE GRAMMAR OF LOVE

"But now abideth faith, hope and love, these three, and the greatest of these is love." [92]

Ever since Paul uttered these words,—poet, philosopher, statesman and scientist have pretty much agreed with him that "the greatest of these is love."

Who is there who would not unite in extolling the role of love as preeminent in the great drama of life? And yet if love is so all-important, why is it that there is so much lovelessness in the world? A casual glance at this planet on which we live reveals that there are large areas where love is very much lacking. We see the reign of hatred and strife, the spirit of revenge and retaliation on every side, nation rising up against nation with murderous intent, and within the borders of the same nation, class contending against class, race discriminating against race—and even within the same family, discord between brother and sister, husband and wife, parent and child. Every day we hear the news of battle, murder and sudden death due to human selfishness, cruelty and greed.

If love is so all-important, why is there such lack of it in life? One answer to our question, in my judgment, and it is only a partial answer, of course, is our failure to understand the grammar of love, especially our failure to understand that love is much more of a verb than a noun; that as a verb the active voice is more important than the passive; and that whatever the voice, the mood in which the verb is used is most important of all.

The first lesson, then, in the grammar of love is to understand that love is much more of a verb than a noun.

Love is not something that exists by itself. It is something that takes place between human beings, and even between other living forms of creation. One does not have to wait for love as though it were an object to be received. One can start in loving. It is an outpouring of the mind and spirit. It is a transitive verb that affirms and predicates an important relation between a given subject and a certain object. It expresses action—a way of behaving. It involves deeds, it implies function and performance. In short, love is something that any one can do something about. This is the first lesson to learn.

The second lesson is to understand that the active voice of the verb "to love" is more important than the passive voice—"to be loved." "I *am* loved" is important. O that everyone were able to say, "I am loved by my parents, I am loved by my wife, by my husband, by my children; I am loved by my friends and acquaintances, by the people with whom I work every day, by my employer or employees, as the case may be. I am loved by the Creator of the universe, or I would not have been created." To realize that one is the object of good will and affection is a gloriously wholesome state in which to be. It is an environment which tends to bring out the best in people and helps them to grow into their full stature as human personalities.

But, "*to love*" is even more important than "to be loved." The incoming tide of affection is a beautiful experience, but the outgoing tide is even more beautiful. It is a creative and glorifying experience. It tends to integrate and organize all one's talents and latent possibilities and puts meaning into life, and gives direction to one's efforts and endeavors.

All the world loves a lover, we are told, and no wonder. When a young man's heart goes out in affection he becomes a transformed personality and his mind becomes more aware of certain aspects of life which he had overlooked before. The world takes on a halo, and that which was drudgery before becomes a delight. The same creative, transfiguring experience takes place even when the object of our love is not some lovely and lovable youth, but some helpless and hitherto despised and friendless human being. Kagawa,

180

the great Japanese humanitarian and Christian, received very little affection in his early and formative years. He never knew his mother and his father all but neglected him. But when he grew up to manhood his heart went out in over-flowing sympathy for the under-privileged, under-nourished, neglected poor of Japan's crowded slums, and in trying to redeem them, he himself found redemption.

All out-going personalities throughout history have testified by their own lives to the supreme value of love in the active voice as over against the passive.

They did not give up loving when they were not loved in return. This was especially true of the great lovers of all time who have been celebrated in song and poetry. While we all needed a great deal of being loved when we were in our infancy and childhood, it is both natural and normal on arriving at youth and adulthood to experience love as giving more than getting, as desiring to serve and care for than to be served and cared for. It is surely evidence of infantilism and spiritual sickness when an adult finds himself more concerned in getting love than in giving it.

A recent editorial by Clifford E. Carpenter underscores this point. He writes:

> If the songs of a nation are a more accurate index of its state of health than its laws, a diagnosis based on much of the popular music emitted by radio and juke boxes would reveal we're a pretty sick country. One who tunes in is likely to hear the plaintive calls of a baby asking for love: 'I want,' 'give me,' 'need you.' An expert who has analyzed modern music says that almost without exception such songs are pathetic cries for attention, for protection, for comfort, for assurance—all pleas reflecting the needs of an infant.[93]

No, to be truly in love as an adult is to want to give as much attention, protection, comfort, and assurance to the one loved as possible without measuring what is returned.

Again, there is another lesson in grammar which we should try to master, and that is that whatever the voice, whether

181

active or passive, the mood in which the verb "to love" is expressed makes all the difference in the world.

There is, first of all, the indicative or declarative mood,— "I love you and I am loved by you." Both are simple statements. How short the words are. How little time it takes to say them, and yet how often we fail to make the effort to do so, but what a difference their utterance can make! We all ought to declare our affection and good will much more frequently than we do, to indicate by words and deeds both the fact that we love and the fact that we know that we are loved, for both are spiritually and socially creative factors making for great joy and happiness in life. In this respect few of us begin to declare ourselves half enough.

The world is a Tower of Babel today. There is widespread confusion because there is a confusion of tongues. But let the indicative mood of the verb *"to love"* be expressed in any language and the confusion would subside for few would fail to understand. The interrogative mood of the same verb, however, is a dangerous one. Does he love me? Do I love him? Or do you love me? Do I love you? This is not so good. Indeed it is a very bad mood into which to fall. It suggests an atmosphere of doubt, suspicion and fear. It tends to destroy the very values which it would create. It was by no accident of speech that the Apostle Paul linked faith and love together for *to love* or to *be loved* means to have faith. We cannot help falling into the interrogative mood sometimes, but it is a spiritually arid mood at best and we should endeavor to get out of it as soon as possible.

The subjunctive mood is even worse. "If you would love me, I would love you, or, if I were loved by you, you would be loved by me." No, this is very bad. It is good English, but poor ethics and poorer psychology. It introduces the jarring thought of barter. A tolerable bargain may be struck between two people, but no joyous partnership can be built on conditional "ifs" and "weres." Many a marriage has been broken up because husband and wife, parents and children, have allowed their affection for one another to become contingent and subjunctive.

The optative mood of our verb is much better, but it too

has its perils. "O that I were loved! Would that I could have something or some one to love!" The urge *to love* and *be loved* is so strong in the human heart that it has often led to tragic blunders. Frustrated in finding adequate and wholesome outlets of expression, it has been often perverted, misdirected and foolishly inverted. Think of the starved and stunted spiritual life of those who try to subsist entirely on the affection of one animal pet or another when there are any number of people who would be only too glad to share their fellowship. Think of the amount of ardency wasted in support of ephemeral causes! Think of the adoration lavished at the clay feet of today's false gods! Youths by the millions expending their divine energy and fervor in crusades which are literally doomed to fail because they should. O what disillusionment is bound to follow! Love in the optative mood is more creative than either the interrogative or subjunctive. Hope as well as faith is joined in Paul's trinity of values, but we must be on guard lest it betray us into reaching after utterly inadequate or spiritually stultifying objects of devotion.

Finally, there is one more mood which we need to understand, namely, the imperative. This is the most difficult lesson of all to learn.

"Thou shalt love the Lord thy God with all thy heart, and with all thy soul, and with all thy mind. This is the first and great commandment. And the second is like unto it, thou shalt love thy neighbor as thyself." [94]

"Ye have heard that it hath been said, Thou shalt love thy neighbor and hate thine enemy. But I say unto you, love your enemies, bless them that curse you, do good to them that hate you, and pray for them that despitefully use you and persecute you." [95]

"Husbands love your wives, even as Christ also loved the church. . . ." [96] and (let) the wife see that she reverence her husband." [97]

How can love of neighbor or enemy, how can love of husband and wife, how can love of even God be a thing commanded? Is not love entirely outside the province of the imperative? This is what a false philosophy has led some

183

of us to believe, but this is not what religion teaches. No, love is not merely a matter of emotion. It is also a matter of will and thought. It is made up of determination as well as sentiment, of resolution as well as feeling, of loyalty as well as liking, of purpose as well as passion. Its other name indeed is good will or benevolence.

This statement may seem to contradict what has been said in earlier chapters about love as an idealizing power not subject to the human will. But here love is being stressed as obedience to that idealizing power and as such it is clearly subject to the human will. As Shakespeare declares, "Love is not love which alters when it alteration finds."[98] When genuine it is marked by constancy and perseverance.

"Love suffereth long, and is kind; love vaunteth not itself, is not puffed up, doth not behave itself unseemly, seeketh not its own, is not provoked, taketh no account of evil; rejoiceth not in unrighteousness but rejoiceth with the truth; beareth all things, believeth all things, hopeth all things, endureth all things. Love never faileth." [99]

When the late Eugene V. Debs, several times a candidate for the presidency, was imprisoned in the Federal Penitentiary at Atlanta, Georgia, he heard about a fellow prisoner being held in solitary confinement, a Negro, serving a life sentence for murder, who had given his guards so much trouble that he was looked upon as hopelessly incorrigible. Mr. Debs asked for the privilege of being taken to the Negro's cell and when he saw him he called him "brother" and kissed him. The Negro looked down in tears and declared that this was the first time in his life that any one had treated him with kindness. As I understand it, that incorrigible one under the magic influence of Mr. Debs' personality became a transformed individual and eventually one of the "trusties" of the penitentiary. Such love surely required an effort of the will and imagination. This kind of love is something that can be commanded, whether directed toward one's wife, one's husband, one's neighbor or even one's enemies.

The God of all the great seers and prophets of the ages speaks to a weary and strife-torn world in the mood imperative—"Thou shalt love," and we disobey to our peril and the peril of unborn generations.

Our vital unity with all men everywhere is the essence of religious faith.

Rich and poor, wise and simple, strong and feeble, we are all joined together by some mystic Oneness whose source we may never know, but whose reality we can never doubt.

The precious life that is in you and me is the same in all.

When one suffers we all suffer.

When one tramps the streets in search for work, we all tramp the streets.

When one hungers for bread, we all hunger.

When one falls before the wintry blast, we all fall.

When one defrauds a fellowman, we all are implicated.

When one destroys a human life, we all share the guilt.

When one ascends the throne of happiness, we all receive its crown.

We *are* our brother's keeper, because that brother is but our larger self.

This mystic identity of the one with the many is a profound truth, most clearly divined by Hosea, Buddha, Jesus and St. Francis, but glimpsed by nearly all the other great seers and prophets of mankind.

Behold, thou shalt love thy neighbor as thyself, because thy neighbor *is* thyself.

Part III

MEDITATION

CHAPTER 23

THE WONDER OF LIFE

O thou, who art the wondrous life behind our own,

Whose presence within ourselves we identify as the creative power of Faith and Hope and Love,

We are moved to address thee in prayer.

Because thy infinite life within us is known unto us immediately and directly,

Without the interposition of any of our physical senses,

Thou art nearer to us than breathing and hearest our prayer even before we ask.

Teach us, we beseech thee, what it means to pray.

We dare to surmise not only that all men pray, whether they realize it or not,

But that all men pray without ceasing;

That they are what they are today largely because of their prayers of yesterday,

And tomorrow they will be what they will be, largely because of their prayers of today.

May we understand that prayer is not necessarily what we say with our lips,

Nor what we consciously think with our minds,

Nor the wish, nor the sigh, nor the aspiration of the moment,

But rather the soul's sincere desire, uttered or unexpressed,

The longing which we entertain in the very depths of our being

Which, when persistently entertained, is bound eventually to affect the course and content of our lives.

May we further understand that all such prayers,

Whether wise or foolish, whether spoken or unspoken,

Are always answered, sooner or later, because of the very
   nature of things,
If not by some outward and visible change,
Then by some inward, intangible alteration within ourselves.
Help us to see that it therefore behooves us
To consider seriously what it is that we should desire,
Lest we be found to be praying for our own impoverishment
   or enslavement.
Teach us that the highest prayer we can pray is for wisdom
To discern more clearly—
And the will to follow more closely—
Thy basic laws,
Concerning the relations of our life to the body, which it
   animates,
Concerning our relations to our fellow man, and
Concerning our relations to the rest of the universe.
Above all, help us to see the folly of trying to use prayer
   as an escape from the consequences of our own actions and
   decisions.
May we have the wit to surmise that there is no permanent
   escape,
That in the end we are punished by our sins and blunders, not
   for them.
And now throughout the rest of this service of worship
May we keep our minds open to whatever truth may come
   to us,
No matter whence it comes, nor whether it confirms or
   contradicts what we have thought before,
So that when we leave this place today,
We may feel that our vision has been enlarged, our purposes
   exalted,
And our hearts warmed toward one another and all mankind.

CHAPTER 24

THE GARMENT OF HOLY IDEALS

Once more, within this beautiful and beloved sanctuary made sacred by many tender memories of those who once worshipped with us, we would renew our confidence in those eternal things in life that outlast life itself.

Here we would put on the garment of holy ideals: partake of the bread of high resolve; refill the vessels of our spiritual courage; and offer a prayer of thanksgiving for the glorious privilege of being alive in such an age as this when so many of the wonders of this universe are being disclosed by science for the first time.

Grant us, O Divine Spirit, something of the radiance and ecstasy of those who have been able to put all foolish doubts aside and truly recognize that the process of creation is still going on before their very eyes.

Grant us something of the shining glory that comes to those who are inwardly assured that life is a house of many mansions and that our brief span of earthly existence is but one room in that house. Therefore teach us to number our days that we may apply our hearts unto wisdom.

Teach us to drink with awe this wondrous cup of experience—to crowd into each day as much awareness as its hours can hold—to treasure our loved ones as the most precious gift which life has to offer.

Teach us also how to give increasing heed to the still small voice that seeks to speak to us from within ourselves above the din of a busy and strident world, and help us to achieve the humility of the child-like mind that through its lowly portals we may enter the Kingdom of Heaven, here and now.

CHAPTER 25

OUR MYSTERIOUS PILGRIMAGE

We turn to this sanctuary of worship as to an inn for wayfaring men, for all of us are fellow pilgrims in a mysterious procession that presses steadily on from birth to death, from an irretraceable past to an unpredictable future.

Some of us are faint and weary and welcome this Sabbath respite to renew our strength and compose ourselves; others are restless with ambition to be on our way.

Some of us are handicapped by the constraints and infirmities of age; others are vibrant with the vigor and eagerness of youth.

Some of us are saddened by the sorrows and frustrations of life; others are buoyant with present and prospective joys.

Many of us are long-time friends, a few of us strangers to the rest, but all of us are bound together by the common hope of being able to complete our mysterious pilgrimage in dignity and self-respect.

Here we would shake off the dust of the road, if only for a little while—

To look back on the path over which we have come,

To refresh our minds with recollections of its beautiful vistas,

To reflect on our own narrow escapes from its perils and pitfalls,

To take courage from the moral triumphs which were ours,

And to offer a prayer of thanksgiving for those staunch and stalwart spirits who were once our fellow pilgrims and have since dropped by the way.

Here, too, we would view the distant scene before us and chart the most promising course to pursue.

192

Here we would make sure that our cruse is filled with the oil of faith and our feet shod with the shoes of perseverance.

"Whate'er the future hath of marvel or surprise," we shall not fear but shall press on to our unseen goal with hearts courageous for any fate and hands outstretched to comrades who may need our help along the way.

O wonder of wonders that prompts our mysterious pilgrimage, keep us ever expectant and exultant to our journey's end.

CHAPTER 26

LIFE'S TWO SCHOOLS

O life who art the great teacher of mankind, thou givest us the choice of at least two schools in which to learn.

There is the school of experience, which thou keepest; it is a dear school,

But there are some of us who must go through that school to the very end.

Through sorrow we are taught the meaning of human sympathy;

Through suffering we are led to learn the secret of patience;

Through defeat the virtue of humility;

Through doubt the creative power of faith;

Through loneliness the worth of friendship;

Through toil the value of leisure;

Through sickness the blessing of health;

Through darkness the glory of light.

Grant that sooner or later we may graduate into the higher school of accumulated knowledge, which Thou also keepest,

Where we may learn directly from the experience of others, without the necessity of going through the same experience ourselves.

Help us to realize that there is a wisdom that the centuries have garnered which we can make our very own;

A wisdom which speaks to us with age-tested assurance, telling us that—

True happiness is not to be gained by much seeking, but only comes as a by-product of unselfish living;

That work, joyously and painstakingly performed, pays
the surest dividends;
That an open mind is the highway to truth;
That reverence is the key to understanding the riddle of
the universe;
That out of the heart proceedeth the issues of life;
That both the Kingdoms of Heaven and Hell are within
the human soul;
And that good will and good faith are the most powerful
forces for overcoming evil in the world.

Open our eyes. O life, our teacher,
To this sifted wisdom of the ages,
Lest we be called hence before we have truly learned
to live!

CHAPTER 27

THE SIMPLE DELIGHTS OF LIFE

O life of our life and life of the world, Thou art the source not only of the great and conspicuous blessings of existence but also of those less obvious benefactions which minister to our needs and make us happy.

How much of our joy and satisfaction comes from the little things of this earth!

We thank Thee for simple delights and evanescent pleasures as well as life's greater gifts—

For the tang of winter air,
For the delicate beauty of gently falling snow,
For the cozy warmth of a crackling fire on the hearth,
For the spiritual radiance cast by the coming holiday season,
For the lovely wistfulness of a fading and dying year,
For the snug privacy of longer loitering evenings,
For the magnetic touch of friendly hands,
For the soft music of mellow voices,
For the healing power of smiling eyes,
For the mystic benediction of a welcome but unexpected guest,
For the precious joy of hearing from loved ones far away,
For the keen satisfaction of suddenly recalling a name long out of mind whose remembrance is sweet,
For the lingering fragrance of former days and friendships which fills this temple of prayer with incense of the spirit.

These intangible and simple delights are after all the greater blessings.

They brighten our pathway and lift from our shoulders many of the burdens of life.

Help us, O life of our life, to realize that this earth is full of spritely messengers of joy and gladness, if we had but eyes to see and ears to hear and hearts to understand.

Grant us wisdom enough not to overlook the little things which do so much to make up the worthfulness of life.

CHAPTER 28

THE "TEN COMMANDMENTS OF SCIENCE"

1. I am TRUTH, the God of SCIENCE, who hath brought thee out of the land of ignorance, out of the bondage of superstition. Thou shalt have no other loyalty before me.

2. Thou shalt not make unto thee any final image of the TRUTH, nor any fixed dogmas concerning the heavens above or the earth beneath or the waters under the earth. Thou shalt not bow down thyself to them nor serve them for I, the TRUTH, am an exacting deity, visiting the stupidities of the fathers upon the children unto the third and fourth generations of them that distrust me and showing enlightenment unto thousands of them that love me and keep my commandments.

3. Thou shalt not take the name of SCIENCE in vain for the God of Science will not hold him guiltless who taketh his name in vain.

4. Remember my Sabbath days to keep them holy, not the days wherein I rested from my labors but the days wherein I made my sublimest achievements.

5. Honor thy sons and daughters and their sons and daughters so that the days of posterity may be made more abundant by the civilization which I can give to them through thee.

6. Thou shalt not murder a fact.

7. Thou shalt not adulterate the blood stream with idiocy, imbecility or insanity.

8. Thou shalt not steal from thy fellow men by concealing thy real convictions or withholding from them important discoveries.

9. Thou shalt not bear false witness against those who claim to be my prophets, nor bring trumped-up charges

against them, nor force them to recant, nor stone them nor persecute them in any way for some of them may be my prophets.

10. Thou shalt not despise thy neighbor because of his religious beliefs nor because of his political opinions, nor because of his economic views, nor because of any conviction which is thy neighbor's for thy neighbor may have some important truth to teach thee and all mankind.

CHAPTER 29

THE SPIRIT OF YOUTH

The spirit of youth is the hope of the world!

What is the spirit of youth?

'Tis the spirit of the lover who sees and glorifies the beauty in another's life.

'Tis the spirit of the adorner who takes a wholesome and self-respecting concern for his own personal appearance.

'Tis the spirit of the crusader who goes forth to champion some high and holy cause.

'Tis the spirit of the explorer who never feels so much at home as in unfamiliar territory.

'Tis the spirit of the prodigal who spends generously of strength and substance on some venture of grand desire.

'Tis the spirit of the troubadour who would bring poetry and music into the drabness of human existence.

'Tis the spirit of the dreamer who dares to look forward to a better world for all mankind.

Whether one be ninety or nineteen, one may possess the spirit of youth.

The spirit of youth is the hope of the world.

CHAPTER 30

PERSISTENT PROBLEMS

The problem of politics is how to spread pre-election enthusiasm throughout the year.

The problem of peace is how to apply the fervor of war to the technique of international cooperation.

The problem of social ethics is how to preserve the conscientiousness of private industry in public enterprise.

The problem of personal development is how to carry the idealism of youth into maturity and age.

The problem of marriage is how to retain the deferences of the courtship amidst the practicalities of wedded life.

The problem of education is how to preserve a child's natural curiosity for knowledge while still trying to satisfy it.

The problem of religion is how to project Sabbath day inspiration into week day affairs.

None of these problems is likely to be solved by the introduction of improved mechanisms alone.

Their ultimate solution lies in the character and skill of individuals.

CHAPTER 31

THE FUNCTION OF THE CHURCH

The main function of the church is a prophetic one. It is the task of bringing about new hearts in men, and a new order in society—

New hearts in which good will, generosity, sincerity and courage shall predominate;

A new order in which peace, justice, freedom, and righteousness shall be established.

It is the task of spiritualizing every department of human life;

Our business, by making service rather than profit the prime objective of commerce and industry,

Our politics, by infusing into men a sense of loyalty to the spirit as well as to the machinery of democracy,

Our juridical system, by introducing sympathy and mercy into the inflexibility of law and precedent,

Our penal institutions, by substituting reformation for retribution as the aim of imprisonment,

Our churches, by making religious tolerance a primary ecclesiastical virtue,

Our schools, by insisting upon full academic freedom for all teachers and professors throughout the land,

Our homes, by making it possible for parenthood to be deliberate and voluntary,

Our foreign relations, by making arbitration and conciliation the only legitimate means of settling international disputes.

This is the task to which the church dedicates its resources, mind, and heart.

CHAPTER 32

COLLECTS

1. To look for the God of the universe without finding first the God within ourselves is to look in vain. God is the power, not ourselves but within us, that makes for truth, beauty and righteousness. Our purpose is to recognize the God within us, that we may better serve his kingdom here on earth.

2. Wherever men gather to seek the highest truth and the wider good, in whatsoever place or clime—whether in the great temple of nature or within the sanctuary of worship, or under the auspices of the forum of contending ideas—that place is holy ground. Let us here join the company of those who seek the highest truth and the wider good.

3. Once more we have come to that season of the year which the traditions of many lands and many centuries have set aside for communion with "the better angels of our nature." Let us join the millions before us—Egyptian, Grecian, Roman, Norseman, Christian and Jew—who, with varying custom and ceremony, have observed this period of the winter solstice as an occasion for joyous celebration. Let us, like them, use this propitious time to re-light the candles of our courage and give voice to our holiest hopes and aspirations.

4. O Thou who hast inspired the festivals of Christmas and Hanukka for the joy and exaltation of mankind, we pray that the sacred light of Bethlehem's star may join with the sacred light of Hanukka's candles to make clearer the path which all men and nations must take to achieve enduring peace and freedom.

5. We lift up our hearts in gratitude and praise for the wondrous gift of life and awareness, for the mighty marvel

of nature's resurrection still hidden beneath the snows of winter, for man's courage to face the mystery of death, and for "the hope that springs eternal in the human breast."

6. In all religions it is a vital part of true worship to hold communion with the saints and prophets who have gone before. We, too, would worship truly. Let us, therefore, turn our minds and hearts toward the saints and prophets who have done so much to make our country what it is. Let us commune with those who, in the moral crises of our nation's life, saw clearly their duty and had the courage to do it.

7. To place a flower, to light a candle, to say a prayer, or to do anything special in memory of the beloved dead is one of the beautiful rites common to all religious faiths—an outward and visible sign of an inward and spiritual grace.

8. With some of our friends and loved ones, it is the voice fully as much as the countenance and sometimes more than the countenance that keeps vivid and fresh our remembrance of them. Blessed are we when these voices still speak to us.

9. O Thou who seest into the deep recesses of the human soul, help us to become truly acquainted with ourselves. Teach us to search our hearts for those hidden and disguised motives which impel us to betray our own best interest as well as that of others. Inspire us with a firm determination to fortify the virtues of our friends and loved ones, to undergird the best in them, not undermine it, and in all other endeavors to preserve that which we most highly cherish.

For we would build up, not tear down, we would create and not destroy.

CHAPTER 33

A CHRISTMAS-HANUKKAH SALUTATION TO ISRAEL

Hail Israel, mother of both the Maccabean and the Nazarene!

We, who at this season celebrate the birth of the one in Christmas psalm and carol, greet thee as thou markest the triumphs of the other in thy Festival of Lights.

Our salutation is one of mingled joy and penitence.

We rejoice that after many centuries of tragic wandering, thy weary feet at last have found a resting place in the land of thy fathers.

How incredible must seem today's consummation of thine ancient dream, and scarcely less incredible the world's mounting admiration of thy valor and tenacity of faith!

Looking back over thy long and toilsome pilgrimage, we who claim fellowship with the Nazarene, the Prince of Peace, recall with shame how oft we have denied fellowship and peace to thee of whom he was begotten.

Forgive, we pray, the terrors and pitfalls by which we have beset thy path.

Forgive the inhumanities and immemorial woes so callously inflicted upon thy defenceless children.

Forgive the spiritual blindness that permitted the countless persecutions and pogroms.

Today, with clearer vision, we would atone for all past wrongs, in part, by sharing with thee not alone thy present joys but thy present sorrows as well, and thy hopes for years to come.

May thy homes which once greeted the Star of Bethlehem with candle-lighted windows be radiant once more with a new and wondrous light.

May thy deserts rejoice and blossom as the rose, and wells of water spring up from the parched ground.

May violence be heard no more in thy land, nor wasting nor destruction within thy borders.

Until once again thy mountains and valleys shall become a land of promise.

Until once again out of Zion shall go forth the law and the word of the Lord from Jerusalem, and He shall judge between the nations and arbitrate for many peoples.

CHAPTER 34

THE NEW YEAR

To face the coming year and all its mystery in a spirit of wholesome reverence;

To meet whatever vicissitudes it brings with fortitude and poise of soul;

To seize upon its opportunities with eagerness and high resolve;

To profit from whatever lessons it has to teach us, opening our minds to the truth that makes men free and our hearts to the truth that makes men happy;

To grow steadily in grace and wisdom;

To become masters of our physical and emotional selves;

To practice patience and self-control amidst the press and strain of life;

To reverence the spirit of reverence in others rather than the object of their reverence;

To be ready at all times to remold our beliefs and opinions at the command of changing experience;

To keep abreast of the best thought of our day—neither rejecting nor accepting the new because it is new, but rather proving all things, holding fast to that which is good;

To extend gradually but not grudgingly the circumference of our friendly interests until no man shall feel himself to be a stranger in our presence;

And finally, to live beyond the immediate present, drinking deeply of the past's inspiration and the future's flowing fountains.

This is our soul's sincere desire.

This is our New Year's prayer.

CHAPTER 35

A RIGHT SPIRIT WITHIN US

O Thou who are infinite in wisdom, in whose life we live and move and have our being, grant us the humility to recognize the finite character of our own wisdom, however great it may seem to be.

May we have the wit to surmise how all men, including ourselves are tempted at times to usurp the role of omniscience and play God to other people and how few of us ever acknowledge even to ourselves its utter presumptuousness.

May we understand that "the impulse to reform the world does not necessarily give us the credentials to be entrusted with the task, but only the signal to begin that reformation within ourselves."

May we, therefore, use this hour of worship to examine into our own minds and hearts to see whether we may not be more a part of the world's present problems than their solution.

May we be moved to inquire to what extent may we be serving the forces of darkness and confusion, rather than the forces of truth and righteousness—to ask ourselves how honestly can we disclaim all responsibility for the attitudes and emotions that precipitate wars and rumors of war—how brave have we been in our support of the agencies making for peace and reconciliation among the nations.

If we are not aware of having directly and overtly encouraged evil by active cooperation, in what degree have we neglected to discourage it by our silence and indifference?

O Thou who are the God behind all nations and religions, quicken thou our imaginations to comprehend:

How much more important it is for us to be right than
to set our neighbor right—

How vain has been our worship if we go from this place today more inclined to remind some one else of his duties, than to remind ourselves of our own—

And how tribal and parochial is the deity we envisage, if we are moved to point out the sins and shortcomings of other peoples and nations, before repenting and rectifying our own.

Unite us, therefore, in a common purpose characterized by righteousness and not the self-righteousness, which has brought about the decline and fall of many a nation in the past.

Once more we would severally pray the ancient prayer: "Create in me a clean heart, O God, and renew a right spirit within me."

CHAPTER 36

THE WONDROUS SILENCES OF LIFE

Amidst the clang and clamor of a bustling world, we would pause a moment to seek the power and poise which comes from quietude. We would lift up grateful hearts for the wondrous silences of life.

For the quietness of the starry heavens above, where no voice is heard;

For the stillness of a deep forest when no leaf is stirring;

For the calmness of a great sea, when all waves are at rest;

For the solemnity of a vast desert where no life is found;

For the breathless wonder evoked by some awe-inspiring chasm of mature, or majestic mountain height;

For the silence of gently falling snow;

For the hush of a house of prayer when one notes the presence of a lone worshipper;

For the peacefulness of an infant deep in slumber;

For the serenity of an aged couple who have weathered the storms of life together, and need no speech nor language;

For the noiseless tread within our thoughts of those whom we "have loved long since, and lost awhile";

For the muted voice within which whispers, "Be still and know that I am God."

Chapter 37

TWO PROPHETS OF FREEDOM

Invocation offered at the unveiling of bronzes of
Susan B. Anthony and Thomas Paine
Hall of Fame, New York, May 18, 1952

O Thou who art the Wondrous Life behind our own, we thank Thee that Thou hast raised up prophets and leaders of the people in all ages and climes, to give counsel and instruction by their understanding and foresight.

We thank Thee especially for the leadership of the illustrious ones whose valiant service in the cause of human freedom we commemorate today.

May we be mindful of the fact that there was a time when the name of neither evoked the reverent acclaim that has now become the obvious due of both.

We pray that we may achieve—something of their sustained devotion to the common good; something of their moral capacity to face scorn and ridicule in order to bear witness to life's deepest insights and highest ideals; something of their persistency of purpose not to be turned aside from a great task whose urgency has been clearly discerned.

Help us to understand that if we would truly honor their memory today, it is not enough for us to praise what they once did and follow safely the trails which they once blazed, but that we too must demonstrate the same adventurous spirit and become the blazers of new trails for our own day and generation.

May we realize that we celebrate in vain unless we are moved to inquire on what hazardous front would they be likely crusading were they living at this fateful hour in human history.

O Thou who didst inspire thy servant, Thomas Paine,

to include the rights of woman in his "Rights of Man," and who didst raise up thy handmaiden, Susan B. Anthony, to emancipate man through her emancipation of woman, show us the next great good that now is not, but ought to be, and grant us the will to lead the way; so that we too may leave behind us some trail of courage, some blaze of freedom, some mark of nobleness; that others coming after us may have reason to take hope and perchance to bless us for having gone before. Amen.

CHAPTER 38

ONE PHALANX OF FAITH

Prayer offered at the service in celebration of "The Liberal
Tradition" of "The Unitarian-Universalist Association,"
Boston, May 14, 1961

Unto the Wondrous Life behind our own, we lift up
grateful hearts for the glorious privilege of being alive in
such an age as this: an age when every institution of human
society is being weighed in the balance and the shape of
things to come is being hammered out on a mighty anvil; an
age when history is being made on a grand and awesome
scale and a new world is in the throes of coming to birth.

In such an age may ours be the imagination to surmise
that never before has the need for the moral imperative of
ethical religion been greater than it is today.

O Thou who raisest up prophets and leaders of the people
in every age and generation we invoke thy divine blessing on
this historic occasion as our two prophetic associations join
forces to present a united witness to the world.

Thus at last has been fulfilled a dream long cherished in
our midst.

May whatever difficulties that must yet be overcome to
fashion us into one effective mission be viewed in the light
of the larger good to be gained.

Having burned our bridges behind us, so to speak, may
we not be tempted to look back with regret but inspired to
look forward with resolve.

As we take courage from the sturdy example of those
brave comrades who once fought the good fight of faith by
our side but are no longer with us except in spirit, may we
also take courage from the re-inforcement of our ranks by

these new recruits before us who offer themselves as instruments of thy divine purpose.

From henceforth may we all move forward together as one phalanx of faith—

To challenge the general authoritarian trend of our times by showing that it is possible to achieve a common program and discipline without sacrificing individual freedom of belief;

To search out and uphold as our own the truth to be found in all religions;

To arouse the conscience of mankind from its sluggish complacency in the presence of immemorial wrongs;

To champion the rights of first class citizenship for all people, both within our own country and throughout the world;

To summon men and nations to give up the insanity of war in this nuclear age before we have mutually destroyed ourselves;

To encourage every feasible step forward to advance the reign of international law and order;

To insure the ultimate triumph of peace and reconciliation by ourselves renouncing those self-righteous attitudes and provocative tactics that necessarily make for strife and violence;

And to proclaim the glad tidings of a new world of enlightenment and abundance for all people that now seems to be within the range of human achievement for the first time in history.

O Thou who art the Divine Discontent behind humanity's present unrest send us forth from this place with the crusading will to make real our heavenly vision of what can and ought to be. Amen.

CHAPTER 39

THE OMEN OF THE ATOM

A strange new light, more luminous by far than Bethlehem's Star, has appeared in the heavens of our time, filling the hearts of men everywhere with fears of what it may portend.

But Wise Men have seen in this light a sign and promise of glad tidings of great joy which shall be to all the people, provided its guidance shall be followed in humility and awe.

Lo! the great light hovers over the United Nations—manger of man's Divine hope of peace on earth.

Let revering kings from near and far bring a treasured portion of their sovereignty to lay at the feet of this holy hope—an infant still in swaddling clothes.

Let wistful shepherds and humble folk in all lands take counsel, not of their fears but of their faith and courage.

Let learned scribes and priests refuse to serve the Herods of empire, that their present schemes of confusion may be worse confounded.

For this is the time long awaited, foretold by seers and prophets of old. To men of good will of all races and creeds comes the voice of one that crieth—

"Prepare ye in the wilderness the way of the Lord;
Make straight in the desert a highway for our God."

REFERENCES AND ACKNOWLEDGMENTS

1. Quotation verified in the presence of the author by Emma B. Sweet of Rochester, New York, one-time secretary to Susan B. Anthony.

1a. William Temple. Quoted in *The Churchman*, p. 11, January 1961.

1b. Albert Einstein. *Living Philosophies*. New York: Simon and Schuster, 1930. Quoted in Great Companions, Vol. 2, p. 138. Boston: Beacon Press, 1941.

2. Job 23:3, 8, 9, and Job 9:11.

3. John Burroughs. *Accepting the Universe*. Boston: Houghton, Mifflin and Company. Quoted in *Great Companions*, Vol. 1, p. 41. Boston: Beacon Press, 1927.

4. Psalm 19:1-4.

5. Psalm 8:1, 3-5.

6. Math. 6:28-29.

7. Math. 5:45.

8. Luke 13:25.

9. I Kings 19:9-14.

10. I Kings 19:15-19.

11. William Cowper. *Hymns of the Spirit*, Hymn 244. Boston: Beacon Press, 1937.

12. William James. *Will to Believe and Other Essays*. Quoted in *Great Companions*, Vol. 1, p. 104. Boston: Beacon Press.

13. Laura Bell Everett. "Faith." Quoted in Fred Merrifield, *Modern Verse and Prose*. New York: Charles Scribner's Sons, 1925.

13a. Edna St. Vincent Millay. *Renascence and Other Poems*. New York: Harper and Brothers, 1917.

14. I Cor. 13:13.

14a. Frederick Lucian Hosmer. *Hymns of the Spirit*. Boston: Beacon Press, 1937, p. 58.

15. John Dewey. *A Common Faith*. Hartford: Yale University Press, 1934, pp. 51 and 52.

16. Psalm 139:8-10.

17. Unitarian Lenten Manual, 1939. Boston: Beacon Press, p. 3.

18. A. N. Whitehead. *Science and the Modern World*. New York: The Macmillan Company. Quoted in *Great Companions*, Vol. 2, p. 417. Boston: Beacon Press, 1941.

19. George Bernard Shaw. *The Collected Works of Bernard Shaw*, Vol. 10, p. xxxiv. Epistle Dedicatory, "Man and Superman." New York: William H. Wise and Company, 1930.

20. C. F. Von Weizsacker, tr. Fred D. Wieck. *The History of Nature*. Chicago: The University of Chicago Press. Quoted in Victor Gollancz, *Man and God*. Boston: Houghton Mifflin Company, 1951, pp. 141-42.

21. François M. A. Voltaire. *Epitre a l'Auter du Livredes Trois Imposteurs*, CXI. Quoted in *Bartlett's Familiar Quotations*, p. 1052. Boston: Little, Brown and Company, 1937.

21a. Johann Wolfgang Goethe, tr. by John S. Dwight. Quoted in "1001 Poems" by Henry W. Wells, p. 194. Atlanta: Tupper and Love, 1953.

21b. John G. Whittier. *Unity Hymns and Chorals*. Chicago: The Unity Publishing Company, 1913, p. 160.

22. Psalm 94:9.

23. Hugh Robert Orr. "The Mighty Marvel." Permission given.

24. Eliza Scudder. *Hymns of the Spirit*. Boston: Beacon Press, 1937, p. 81.

24a. Curtis W. Reese. *Hymns of the Spirit*. Boston: Beacon Press, 1937, p. 502.

25. "Yigdal," in *Hymns of the Spirit*. Boston: Beacon Press, 1937, p. 1.

26. *Hymns of the Spirit*. Boston: Beacon Press, 1937, p. 234.

27. Luke 11:8-10.

28. Rufus Ellis. *Sermons*. Boston: Cupples, Upham and Company, 1885, p. 7.

29. *Ibid.*, pp. 1-2.

30. Bertrand Russell. *Power: A New Social Analysis* New York: W. W. Norton and Company, 1938, pp. 14-15.

31. Math. 9:22.

32. George B. Cutten. *Psychological Phenomena of Christianity*. New York: Charles Scribner's Sons, p. 725.

33. Jacob Trapp. *Hymns of the Spirit*. Boston: Beacon Press, 1937, p. 352.

33a. Amos 5:23-24, as translated by Ulysses G. B. Pierce in "Soul of Bible," pp. 254-255. Boston: Beacon, 1914.

33b. Is. 1:13-15.

33c. Mic. 6:6-8.

34. Mark 7:6-7.

35. Is. 1:13-16.

36. Mic. 6:8.

37. Decoration Day Oration, 1882, in *Works of Robert Ingersoll*, Vol. IX. C. P. Farrell Company, 1900, pp. 453-454.

38. James Hastings. *Dictionary of the Bible* (Extra Vol.) New York: Charles Scribner's Sons, 1904, Item 30 on p. 347.

39. Thomas Carlyle. *Past and Present*. Quoted in C. Griswold Williams, *Antiphonal Readings for Free Worship*. Boston: The Murray Press, 1933, p. 9.

40. Romans 7:24.

41. Job 31:25.

42. II Kings 5:18.

43. Ph. 4:11.

44. Psalm 122:1.

45. A. J. H. Duganne. Quoted in *Social Hymns*. New York: The A. S. Barnes Company, 1914, p. 54.

46. Vachel Lindsay. *The Congo*. Quoted in *Great Companions*, Vol. 1, p. 487. Boston: Beacon Press, 1927.

47. H. G. Wells. *The Outline of History*. New York: Macmillan Company, 1920.

48. Miles Poindexter. *The Ayar-Inkas*. New York: Horace Liveright, 1930.

49. Edwin Markham. "The Place of Peace," in "Poems by Edwin Markham," p. 90. Selected by Charles L. Wallis. New York: Harper and Brothers, 1950.

50. Luke 23:34.

51. John 18:38.

52. James 4:17 (Revised Standard Version).

53. Acts 22:20.

54. George Seldes. *The Great Quotations*. New York: Lyle Stuart, 1960, p. 129.

55. *Ibid.*, p. 629.

56. Psalm 51:1-4, 6, 10.

56a. Math. 7:1-2.

57. John 8:7.

58. Bertrand Russell. *A Free Man's Worship.* Quoted in C. Griswold Williams. *Antiphonal Readings for Free Worship.* Boston: Murray Press, 1933, p. 72.

59. *The Ballad of Reading Gaol* in *Works of Oscar Wilde*, National Library. Boston: The Wyman-Fogg Company, 1909, p. 345.

60. II Sam. 18:33.

61. Address by David Rhys Williams on "Church of the Air," Columbia Broadcasting Company, June 15, 1950, under title "How We Destroy the Thing We Love."

62. David Rhys Williams. *World Religions and the Hope for Peace.* Boston: Beacon Press, 1951, p. 56.

63. William Shakespeare. "Measure for Measure," Act II, Sc. 2, line 117.

64. Richard Chenevix French. Quoted in *Hymns of the Spirit*. Boston: Beacon Press, 1937, p. 276.

65. *Maxims of Rochefoucauld.* Quoted in "The New Dictionary of Thoughts." New York: Classic Publishing Company, 1934, p. 241.

66. I Cor. 13:11.

66a. Tao-Te-King XLIX. Taoist Scriptures. There are several translations. See "Bible of the World" by Robert O. Ballou. New York: Viking Press, 1939, p. 491. See also "Tongues of Fire," by Grace E. Turnball. New York: Macmillan Company, 1929, p. 164.

66b. John Haynes Holmes, *et al. Readings from Great Authors.* New York: Dodd, Mead and Company, p. 89.

67. Mark 3:23-24 (Revised Standard Version).

68. Rom. 12:21.

69. Deut. 5:15.

70. Ex. 20:11.

71. "Farewell Speech," by Dwight D. Eisenhower, January 17, 1961. Quoted in "U.S. News and World Report," January 30, 1961, p. 69.

72. Edwin Markham. *Man-Making.* Quoted in *Quotable Poems*, Vol. I. Chicago: Willet Clark Company, 1928, p. 71.

73. Walter A. Cutter. "Loyalties." Quoted in *Quotable Poems*, Vol. II, Chicago: Willet Clark Company, 1931, p. 41.

74. Psalm 133:1.

75. Math. 10:34-36.

76. Math. 26:52.

77. Luke 3:14.

78. Job 14:14.

79. "Death and Old Age," by Cicero, born 106 B.C. Quoted in M. J. Savage, *Minister's Handbook.* Boston: George E. Ellis, 1906, p. 60.

80. I Cor. 15:50.

81. "The Wisdom of Solomon," in Ulysses G. B. Pierce. *The Soul of the Bible.* Boston: Beacon Press, 1914, p. 272.

82. *Ibid.*, pp. 272-273.

83. J. B. Rhine. *New World of the Mind.* New York: William Sloane Associates, 1953, p. 54.

84. *Ibid.*, p. 52.

85. *Ibid.*, pp. 242-243.

86. *Ibid.*, p. 243.

87. Quotation verified and permission given by Swami Akhilananda of The Ramakrishna Vedanta Society, Boston.

87a. Charles Richet. *Thirty Years of Psychical Research.* Tr. from the French by Stanley De Brath. New York: The Macmillan Company, 1923, pp. 7-8.

88. *Hymns of the Spirit.* Boston: Beacon Press, 1937, p. 252.

88a. Sermons by A. Powell Davies in All Souls Church, Washington, D.C., 1956. Quotation verified and permission given by Mrs. A. Powell Davies.

89. Alfred Tennyson. "In Memoriam," Part XCVI, Stanza 3.

90. William Wordsworth. "Ode upon the Intimations of Immortality," opening lines.

91. Rabindranath Tagore. "Sadhana." New York: The MacMillan Company, 1913, p. 51.

92. I Cor. 13:13 (American Standard Version).

93. Clifford E. Carpenter. Editorial in *Democrat* and *Chronicle*. Rochester, New York, July 22, 1959. Permission.

94. Math. 22:37-39.

95. Math. 5:43-44.

96. Eph. 5:25.

97. Eph. 5:33.

98. William Shakespeare. Sonnet 116.

99. I Cor. 13:48 (American Standard Version).

The author gratefully acknowledges permission to reprint the foregoing, and wishes to acknowledge additional permissions from: The Christian Century Foundation ("Loyalties" by Walter A. Cutler); Houghton, Mifflin Company ("Faith" by Laura Bell Everett); Norman Millay Ellis ("Renascence" by Edna St. Vincent Millay); the Macmillan Company ("The Congo" by Vachel Linsay); and Virgil Markham ("Man-Making" and "The Place of Peace" by Edwin Markham).

INDEX

Aaron, 50
Abelard, 152
Abraham, 22
Absalom, 106
Adler, Alfred, 98, 154
Agassiz, Louis, 168
Akhilananda, 167
Alexander the Great, 116
Anthony, Susan B., xi, 22, 212
Arnold, Matthew, 22
Arthur, King, 79
Asoka, King, 74, 78
Augustine, 12, 18, 25, 95

Backus, E. Burdette, 22
Bacon, Francis, 152
Bacon, Roger, 12, 152
Ballou, Hosea, 91
Beethoven, Ludwig von, 27
Blatchford, Robert, viii
Browning, Robert, 166
Buddha, Gautama, 65, 89, 111, 113, 114, 116, 174, 185
Burke, Edmund, 96
Burroughs, John, 7
Butler, Samuel, 103

Caesar, Julius, 166
Caiaphas, 94
Calvin, John, 18, 91, 92, 134, 176
Carlyle, Thomas, 69
Carpenter, Clifford, E., 181
Cato, 152
Channing, William Ellery, 91
Churchill, Winston, 156, 157
Cicero, 152, 158, 166
Clay, Henry, 128, 129
Coleman, George W., viii
Columbus, Christopher, 78
Coolidge, Calvin, 90
Confucius, 50, 65, 89
Cowper, William, 10
Crapsey, Algernon S., viii
Cutten, George B., 55

Darrow, Clarence, viii
Darwin, Charles, xv, 160, 163
Davies, A. Powell, 171
David, King, 106
Debs, Eugene V., viii, 184
Descartes, René, 153
Dewey, John, 22
Drummond, Henry, 95

Edwards, Jonathan, 25, 91, 92, 176
Einstein, Albert, 154
Eisenhower, Dwight D., 141
Elijah, 8, 9, 10, 11, 17
Emerson, Ralph Waldo, 46
Epictetus, 152
Ezekiel, x

Ford, Henry, 120
Fosdick, Harry Emerson, viii, 147
Francis of Assisi, 36, 95, 185
Freud, Sigmund, xv, 98, 154

Galileo, 168
Gandhi, Mahatma, 65, 95, 132, 174
Gannett, William C., 72
Garrison, William Lloyd, 147
Gaulle, Charles De, 79

Hillel, 152
Hitler, Adolf, 139, 140
Hosea, 176, 185
Hosmer, Frederick L., 14, 170
Hugo, Victor, 166
Huntington, 162
Huss, John, 147
Huxley, Thomas, 166
Hyslop, James H., 163

Isaiah, 12, 38, 60, 88

James, William, 13, 14, 157
Jefferson, Thomas, 50

222

DATE DUE

SE 20 '63			
DISPLAY			
MR 20 '69			
AP 19 '72			
MY 3 '72			
DE 17 '74			
JA 7 '75			
JA 21 '75			
2-11-75			
FE 25 '75			
AP 6 '94			
GAYLORD			PRINTED IN U.S.A.